DARKNESS INTO LIGHT

Darkness into Light

A Nation's Response

Joan Freeman

BEEHIVE

Published 2022 by
Beehive Books
7–8 Lower Abbey Street
Dublin 1
info@beehivebooks.ie
www.beehivebooks.ie

Beehive Books is an imprint of Veritas Publications

Copyright © Joan Freeman, 2022

ISBN 978 1 80097 030 4

Thank you to the *Mayo News* and the *Meath Chronicle* for granting permission to Beehive Books to reproduce article extracts.

A catalogue record for this book is available from the British Library.

Design and typesetting by Colette Dower, Beehive Books
Cover photo by Gary Ashe, garyashe@gmail.com
Printed in the Republic of Ireland by SPRINT-print Ltd, Dublin

Beehive books are printed on paper made from the wood pulp of managed forests. For every tree felled, at least one tree is planted, thereby renewing natural resources.

This book is dedicated to my four extraordinary children,
Marie, Siobhan, Aislinne and Martin.
You are the link to my past,
the anchor to my present
and the bridge to my future.

Contents

Foreword

It is a privilege for me as Taoiseach to write this foreword marking Darkness into Light. This annual fundraiser in support of the work of Pieta has grown into a worldwide event in just over a decade.

It is truly remarkable that the inaugural walk, with 400 people in the Phoenix Park in 2009, has grown to over 200,000 people taking part in 16 countries across 5 continents.

The walk provides a very special and poignant opportunity for people to connect with others and to show their support for people and communities who have been impacted by suicide.

Suicide is extremely complex and most of the time there is no single event or factor that leads someone to take their own life. But every death by suicide is tragic and leaves devastation in its wake for individuals, family, friends and communities.

I have lost count of the number of people who have shared their very personal experiences of the support offered by Pieta in times of distress. The freely accessible one-to-one counselling for people experiencing suicidal ideation, who self-harm or for people bereaved by suicide are key supports in our collective effort to reduce suicide.

In November 2020 the Minister for Health and the Minister of State for Mental Health and Older People announced the extension of *Connecting for Life: Ireland's National Strategy to Reduce Suicide* to 2024. Reducing suicide is a key government objective, and one that can only be achieved with the participation of, and collaboration with, front-line agencies such as Pieta. They are an important component of our wide range of mental health promotion and suicide prevention initiatives nationwide.

It is so important to always remember that if you are concerned about your mental health or that of someone you know, please reach out for support. Even though it may not always feel that way, support is available – from organisations like Pieta, and many other trusted sources.

To find out more, you can visit www.yourmentalhealth.ie for information on how to mind your mental health, support others or to find a support service in your area. You can also call the YourMentalHealth information line on 1800 111 888 anytime day or night for information on mental health services in your area.

Micheál Martin
Taoiseach

Introduction

I suppose the only way I can introduce this book is by writing about suicide. Not a particularly upbeat way to start, perhaps, but hopefully by the time you have finished this book, you will understand that there is light at the end of a tunnel of darkness; and while we cannot prevent every suicide in our country, we are certainly making an extraordinary effort, through services, individual responses and, of course, the Darkness into Light annual walk. This 5-kilometre walk has grown from small beginnings in the Phoenix Park in 2009 to become a global movement, raising both funds for Pieta House centres and our awareness of suicide, as well as providing a forum for bereaved families to remember their loved ones.

Let's start at the dark side first, and look at the facts. Suicide has been around for thousands of years. The term originated from the Latin word *suicidium*, which means 'killing of oneself'. Approximately 1.5 per cent of all deaths worldwide are by suicide,[1] with rates generally higher among men than among women and generally more common among men over the age of seventy.[2] However, in certain countries in Europe (Ireland being one of them), those between the ages of fifteen and thirty are at the highest risk of suicide.[3] In addition, it's estimated that globally there are ten to twenty million attempted suicides every year.[4] In the Western world, while suicide rates are higher among men, attempts are more common among women.[5]

Historically, in some countries, suicide was seen as a totally acceptable behaviour. In Japan, a form of suicide known as 'hara-kiri' was seen as a respectful way of making up for failure or as a form of protest. In India, the practice of 'sati' was common, where a widow would kill herself by throwing herself on her husband's funeral pyre, either willingly or because she was under pressure from her family or society.

In Ireland, however, both Church and State stood against suicide. In law, suicide and attempted suicide were illegal right up until 1993, when they were decriminalised. As far as the Catholic Church was concerned, suicide was a sin and, until 1966, the person who committed it would not be allowed to be buried in hallowed ground. States, including the Irish State, were just as punitive and unforgiving: 'Indeed, the attitude to suicide up to the nineteenth century could be described as almost vindictive … Up to 1870 the property of a person who had committed suicide was forfeit to the State and it was only in 1882 that the British Parliament outlawed the practice of interring the remains of a person who had committed suicide in a public highway with a stake driven through the body. Nonsensical though it may seem, it was the practice at one time to hang people who had unsuccessfully attempted suicide.'[6] Hence the word 'committed' was always associated with the word 'suicide'; the person had committed a crime and committed a sin. It's no wonder that the subject became taboo and this desperate act became hidden. Suicide is neither a sin nor a crime; it is a tragic act which takes place when a person feels that there is no other way out of their despair.

Since Pieta House opened its first centre in 2006, Ireland has developed a better and more compassionate understanding of suicide. Heretofore, most people would have believed that suicide usually came as a result of someone suffering from a long-term and enduring mental illness. But now we know better:

we have discovered that, while suicide is a complex subject and there is no one reason that lies behind it, most suicides are a result of a reaction to a distressing event or period in a person's life. Before I opened Pieta House, my personal experience and research pointed me in this direction, and then, during the 2008 economic crisis in Ireland, our findings were endorsed. The majority of people who attended the service during those years were men from the building trade or farmers who found it difficult to survive. Their loss of work led to a loss of identity and, unfortunately, this would have a knock-on effect on relationships and family. Their experience would turn into despair. Gathering all this research and information was crucial, because it allowed us to adapt our service around this knowledge. As a result, we created national campaigns such as 'Mind Our Men' and 'Mind ur Buddy' to raise awareness and we tried to educate the nation with the campaign 'The Signs of Suicide'.

These campaigns not only enlightened the public but also were catalysts for acceptance and greater understanding from society. Understanding more about the causes of suicide spurred people on to raise funds for a service that was completely free of charge and required no referral from doctors or psychiatrists. It gave men, women and children the freedom to seek help without any consequences, and their families much-needed insight and support.

It was these very men, women and children who said yes to participating in a walk that began with 400 people in the Phoenix Park in 2009; a walk – and a message – that went global, with over 200,000 people taking part all across the world each year.

This book is dedicated to all the people who were involved in Darkness into Light, whether they were committee members, volunteers, or the staff of Pieta House. I also dedicate it to the thousands of people who rose at the coldest hour of the night, aware that the darkest hour is always before dawn. These people led the battle in the fight against suicide. These Soldiers of the Dawn have brought and will continue to bring this nation from the dark into the glorious light.

NOTES
[1] Seena Fazel and Bo Runeson, 'Suicide', *The New England Journal of Medicine*, vol. 382, 3 (2020), pp. 266–274.
[2] World Health Organization, *Preventing Suicide: A Global Imperative*, Geneva, Switzerland: World Health Organization, 2014, pp. 7, 20, 40, https://www.who.int/publications/i/item/9789241564779; accessed 24 March 2022.
[3] Ibid.
[4] José Manoel Bertolote, and Alexandra Fleischmann, 'Suicide and psychiatric diagnosis: a worldwide perspective', *World Psychiatry*, vol. 1, 3 (2002), pp. 181–5.
[5] Bernard Chang, David Gitlin and Ronak Patel, 'The depressed patient and suicidal patient in the emergency department: evidence-based management and treatment strategies', *Emergency Medicine Practice*, vol. 13, 9 (September 2011), pp. 1–23; quiz 23–4.
[6] Minister for Justice Máire Geoghegan-Quinn, Dáil Éireann debate, Wednesday, 5 May 1993, https://www.oireachtas.ie/en/debates/debate/dail/1993-05-05/20/; accessed 24 March 2022.

CHAPTER ONE

In the Beginning

Although the air was damp, it wasn't cold. I could feel a soft breeze against my face, while at the same time the gentle wind caused the leaves to slightly rustle on the branches above. I was under a tree – holding onto the rough bark, afraid to let go. I was hiding. An overwhelming sense of panic surged through me as I peered around the large trunk to see what I knew was there already: headlights, one after another, relentlessly coming in my direction. I squeezed my eyes shut, hoping that when I opened them again the very same cars would have vanished.

I jumped out of my skin when my daughter Aislinne shouted at me, 'Mum, what are you doing? For God's sake – we have been looking everywhere for you! You are wanted up at the start line. Come on, hurry.' She took my hand and I followed her reluctantly, stumbling and cursing. Within a few minutes, I found myself standing on a makeshift stage looking out over the Phoenix Park, with a microphone in my hand. My hand shook as I brought the mike to my trembling lips. I took a deep breath and with a quivering voice I shouted: 'Good morning! And welcome to the sixth annual Darkness into Light walk!'

It's difficult to know where this story begins. Did it start, for example, in this sixth year, when I was so overwhelmed after I realised how enormous this annual walk was becoming that I wanted to hide? Or was the beginning in May 2009, when we held the event for first time, when around 400 people turned up to a poorly lit Phoenix Park in the middle of the night? These brave, adventurous people arrived not knowing what to expect, but then again, neither did we.

Or maybe the start is my own beginning, my birth, my family – my life, which eventually would lead me to meet these extraordinary strangers who became extraordinary friends. It's as good a place as any to begin this story.

Even though I was born in 1958, I refuse to class myself as a child of the fifties because it conjures up images of the ideal housewife: curled hair, clean, sterile apron, cooking over a hot stove and serving her family, a role which I would be expected to follow. Instead, I like to think of myself as a child of the sixties, a far more exciting era, which in turn conjures up images of miniskirts, wild parties and forward thinking. I may not have been to too many wild parties, but I like the idea that the era in which I was born looked so much to the future.

I was born on 2 April to Marie (née Kelly) and John Lowe. For years, my mother told the story that I appeared in the world not long after midnight, because she'd 'held onto' me, in case I was born on April Fool's Day. I never knew if she was joking or not. My parents were very much people of their time: they married a few months after the end of the Second World War and at first they lived in a cramped flat in a large house on Belgrave Square in Rathmines, Dublin. They were both devout Catholics whose faith helped them through difficult times in their lives. After three years of marriage, the children started arriving. My mother would often say that they 'ordered' eleven babies, but due to miscarriages only eight of those babies survived.

The first years must have been difficult for them. The flat didn't have a kitchen sink, so clothes and dishes had to be washed in the bath. There was only one bedroom – so you can imagine how cramped conditions were when the first baby,

Francis, arrived, followed eighteen months later by twin girls, Catherine and Margaret. By the time they were expecting their fourth baby, John, they had saved, begged and borrowed enough money for a deposit and bought a house on Cromwellsfort Road in Crumlin. It must have been heaven for them: three bedrooms, a proper kitchen and a large back garden. My father was working as a bartender at the time, in the Black Lion pub, while my mother stayed at home looking after the growing brood. Soon after moving in, my brother John was born, followed by my sister Marian. Family life began to take shape and settle.

Then my father was offered the position of manager at Clontarf Castle, which must have seemed like a big step up from his bartending job. This famous building was owned by my grand-aunt on my mother's side, Jenny Egan (nee Kelly). She was the owner of Egan's department store on Henry Street and bought the castle for £28,000 in 1957. To this day, if anyone asks me where I was born, I automatically answer, 'Clontarf.' This is usually followed by, 'Oh really, what part of Clontarf?' I then receive an incredulous look when I tell them that I lived in Clontarf Castle. For a moment, just a moment, I feel like royalty!

However, the reality was far from royal. The place was nothing like it is now. Then, there was just a pub on the ground floor and living accommodation above. The pub would become a popular cabaret venue in the 1970s, but it only became the Clontarf Castle we know today in the 1990s, when it was transformed into a hotel. The family moved in around 1957, having sold the house in Crumlin to my father's sister. It might sound adventurous, and even glamorous, but the building was mouldy and damp; rats used to run riot – and didn't confine themselves to the bar either but would be found scurrying around the living quarters. In hindsight, life would have been easier if my parents and my siblings had remained in the flat in Rathmines. It might have been cramped, but I know that their time at Clontarf Castle was stressful and difficult; in particular, for my father, a gentle and sensitive man, who had found himself trying to run a business for my strong-willed grand-aunt as well as provide for his ever-increasing family.

I came sixth in the family and I can only imagine that having six children under the age of ten would have been the last straw for my parents. We lived in a time when Ireland had its fair share of economic troubles: unemployment was high, forcing people to emigrate, and although my father still had his job in Clontarf, the challenging working and living conditions were proving to be too much. It was then that he became low and despondent. Today, we would understand that he was depressed, but in the 1950s, the condition wasn't acknowledged, for fear of ending up in one of the terrifying mental hospitals of the time, such as Grangegorman.

I now know that his depression was shared by other members of his family, particularly his father, a farmer from Co. Offaly. Famously, my grandfather did not say a single word out loud for two years, following the departure of his youngest child for Dublin. Nowadays, he would seek help, but then, he was alone with his depression and the loneliness of running the farm by himself.

Nonetheless, my mother was astute enough to notice that my father was becoming depressed and to do what she could to help. It was she who suggested that he leave Ireland to look for work in England. This was for practical reasons, of course, as jobs were scarce, but as she would tell me later, when he underwent another period of deep depression, she hoped that a new departure would lift his mood.

In 1959 my father went by boat to England to look for work and for somewhere to live. My mother, having recognised Dad's low mood, feared for his safety. So, she sent my sisters, Catherine and Margaret, with him. While that seems insane now – to give a depressed man, who was supposed to be looking for a job and accommodation in another country, the added responsibility of looking after nine-year-old twins – it was incredibly intuitive of her. She knew he would be focused on looking after Catherine and Margaret. Thankfully, they all arrived safely. They stayed with my mother's sister Joan for a few weeks, while my father looked for work and a home. I'm sure he missed Mum terribly, but in the days before mobile phones, communication was difficult: both he and she would queue at their local public telephone box at exactly the same time for their weekly chat. After establishing work and accommodation, my father returned to Ireland to help move the whole family to England.

In 1959 my parents, my brothers Francis and John, my sisters Catherine, Margaret and Marian, and myself arrived in the UK and began a new life in Warwickshire. It didn't take us long to settle down in England. My father got a job in Lockheed, a factory that built parts for aeroplanes. My mother continued to look after the family and the home and added two more members to the familial group, my sisters Theresa and Mary.

Although now in England, like so many emigrants, my parents still lived in the 'Irish way' with daily Mass and, of course, the rosary every night. I'm sure that, like so many families across Ireland, the prayer session was mainly composed of giggling and silences from the person who was supposed to say the decade. In our case, this behaviour came not just from my siblings but also my mother. My father, who had been raised a strict Catholic, was stern and stoic, insisting on being reverent and respectful. When I grew older, I was the goody two shoes, which meant that inevitably I would be the only one who could finish the prayers without cracking up. This is when I would look smugly at the rest of them, feeling like I was the best out of the lot of them. God, I was full of it!

We were a very typical Irish family in that it was seen as a blessing to have children who joined a religious order. In the years that followed our time in England, my two brothers went to seminaries to become priests and Margaret, my sister, went off to become a nun. Joining a religious order back then was akin to emigrating in many ways: loved ones were lost to their families, joining another family to which they'd belong for the rest of their lives. When Margaret left home, it was the one and only time I saw my father cry. Much later on, when I saw the film *The Nun's Story*, starring Audrey Hepburn as a novice, I thought about that time in our lives when Margaret went into the convent and we were all devastated. In the end, the three of them left during their years of training, before any vows were made, and I know that my parents were overjoyed to have them home again.

It was around this time that my parents decided to come back to Ireland. Even though many of their children were grown and decided to remain in England, Mum and Dad pined for the country they had left eleven years previously. They always felt that they were in a 'foreign land'. I will always remember going to Mass on St Patrick's Day when my parents would have tears running down their faces while they attempted to sing 'Hail Glorious St Patrick'.

We returned to Ireland in June 1970. I was twelve, and I remember it so well, as Dana had just won the Eurovision Song Contest. I started secondary school at St Louis Convent in Rathmines and, although I was quite academic, I found school in Ireland a struggle. For a start, I had an English accent; worse, I had to learn Irish, and every time I would open my mouth to speak it in lessons, the entire class would crack up! Unable to catch up, I became the class messer, dodging homework and doing badly for the next six years. In 1975 I finished school with great joy and delight, and for the following few years worked as a junior secretary in a number of administrative jobs. Life was simple and predictable, and I would hand over the few bob to my parents every week. At that time, only my father and I worked outside the home. Would you believe I was earning more than he was? My two younger sisters were in college, Theresa studying law and Mary studying the arts.

I was twenty when I had my first boyfriend: Des Walsh. He was about two years older than me and had a car, but not only that – he was a bank manager's son. In those days a girl would feel that she'd hit gold if a guy had those two attributes and would brag about it at every opportunity. I was mad about Des and introduced him to all my friends and, of course, I met all of his. Richard Mulcahy was Des's best friend at the time. Although my relationship with Des lasted only about a year, forty years later they would both play an important part in my life. During my campaign for the presidency in 2018, Richard would be my campaign manager and Des became my financial support.

At the tender age of twenty-two, I met Pat Freeman, who became my life partner, husband, best friend and biggest fan. After two years together, we were married on 24 April 1982. Pat had his own business, a grocery shop and post office in the well-established estate of Bluebell in Dublin 12. Like my parents, we began to have children in rapid succession, four in the first five years of marriage. It was a busy time, with both of us running the business and raising our children. When I was first married, I wanted twelve children, but after the first two, realised that they were very hard work! Like Pat, our children, Marie, Siobhan, Aislinne and Martin, would be tireless and unwavering in their support for my work and without them, it would have been so much harder.

I suppose I inherited a positive, can-do attitude from my mother. When I had my last child at thirty, I thought I knew it all. Not only did I know how to be an expert in parenting, but I also thought I knew it all as far as relationships were concerned. I'd seen my mother's emotional skills at work with my father and became interested in the dynamic of a lifelong partnership, so in 1989 I became a couples' counsellor.

A therapist or counsellor is a facilitator who allows issues to be heard and then watches in awe as the majority of couples sort themselves out. At least, that is what I learned. Little did I know when I qualified that being present during a couple's difficulties is not only a privilege, because they trust you with their most intimate problems, but it also opens your eyes to what problems can look like in a marriage or relationship and how you can cope with them.

I could see first-hand how relationship difficulties could impact a person's mental health and I wanted to learn more about it, so I decided to study psychology in greater depth, enrolling at university to study for a bachelor of science (BSc). Unlike in school, where everything had been so hard, I found the discipline easy, because I loved people and the study of human behaviour. I obtained a BSc, and then later a master's in psychology . Studying with four children was interesting. I crammed my work into the weekends, when Pat was off work – and still remember roaring at the children to keep the noise down! See what I mean about a supportive family? Nobody ever complained. The reason I share this with you is because it became a backdrop to my future, providing vital support when I witnessed depression in people I loved and when I dived headlong into a mission to break the mould when it came to mental health and suicide.

Looking back on these early years, I realise how easy my life was. I was married to a kind and loving man, I had four terrific children, we had our own home and I had begun a new career in counselling. Thinking now about my work life at that time, though, it is obvious to me that, whether I was helping people with bereavement, relationship counselling, depression or work problems like bullying, I veered away from serious issues, in particular suicide. If anyone presented themselves to me with enduring psychiatric issues, or I thought they were suicidal, I would send them off to the GP or to A & E straight away. Back then, I felt that suicide was dangerous, both to the person and to me. I shudder to think how ignorant of the subject I was at that time, but I believe now that my behaviour was more than likely shared by the majority of therapists and counsellors. I know that it was built on a foundation of fear. Fear was the brick wall that prevented me from helping people who were experiencing suicidal distress. It was far safer to talk to them about their relationships and to counsel people who were bereaved, but suicide was completely different. I didn't know anyone who had ever attempted suicide, let alone died this way.

This was the early nineties and, believe it or not, still in Ireland no one spoke about depression, or uttered the words 'mental health' (the word 'mental' was only used if it was describing someone in a derogatory way). The word 'suicide' was rarely mentioned. There was still a huge stigma attached to it. Nobody ever died by suicide in Ireland – because, after all, it was a sin as far as the Church was concerned. It was ignored by the government, mainly because it reflected a society that wasn't working. This was the Ireland I lived in, an Ireland I knew and an Ireland I was entirely comfortable with. Having said that, I am sure that there were kind, compassionate therapists and counsellors who were welcoming people who were in acute distress – sadly, at the time, I didn't feel able to be one of them.

* * *

All that changed when a close member of my family took their own life. We were utterly shattered as a family and life would never be the same again. While this horror was the catalyst for change in my own life, I have promised my relative's children that I won't reveal personal details that will result in more pain for them. They would like to remember the person's life with joy, rather than their death with great sadness. And it is not my story to tell; however, I can speak freely about my personal response to this nightmare.

If ever I hear of someone who has died by suicide now, my first thought is of their family and loved ones and what a terrible journey lies ahead of them. No words can describe this journey: despair, darkness, desolation capture it only to a small degree.

The question that everyone who has travelled this route usually begins with is, 'Why?' I know that it was true for me. In truth, it's a question that can never be answered. Instead, for the relatives, it becomes a lonely scream in the dark that nobody hears. It's an inner wail that can never be calmed.

This question is usually followed at breakneck speed by the awful questions, 'Why didn't I spot it?' 'Why didn't I stop it?' If ever I was to give words of comfort to families and friends who have lost someone through suicide, I would tell them in total honesty that the answer to these questions is – because family and friends are the last people to know. In fact, many people will say that their loved one showed absolutely no signs of suicidal intent. They are right; the loved one in distress was trying to protect them.

At the time when my family member died, twenty years ago, I experienced all those emotions, in particular the constant questions, which seemed to be on repeat in my head. I remember that 'why' was the first word I woke up to and the last word I fell asleep to. It's hard to believe now, but the world was a place that still had little technology. We did not have the internet in our home, nor did we have easy access to mobile phones. We could not, at the drop of a hat, google, looking for insights into any topic, never mind suicide. So, my journey to understand what had happened took me to the local library. Every day, after my children went to school, I would book an hour on the internet in the library. I would type in the word 'suicide' and wait to see what came up on to the screen. Truthfully, I was hoping that I would find the words that would reassure me: suicide could not be prevented; what had happened to my relative wasn't my fault. However, to my horror, I read the opposite. While this research verified that family and friends are the last to know when someone is suffering, it described in detail how a society should respond to someone in distress, how doctors, hospitals, therapists, schools, workplaces should be educated. This information highlighted ways to become aware of the signs of suicide and what one should do if the signs are present in someone you love.

I felt an overwhelming sense of guilt. With all deaths there are regrets around not spending more time with the person who died, or being kinder when they were alive, but suicide comes with a particular type of guilt that will forever remain. Regrets circle endlessly: I should have known; I could have prevented it; why didn't I listen harder or take them seriously? Guilt is the one emotion that eats away at your core.

Every day I would surround myself with books and articles on suicide. With every article and every book I read on the subject, however, I was becoming more and more despondent, feeling more and more guilty, because I was learning that the death of the person I was grieving might have been prevented. I became depressed. I was functioning on a basic level. I would continue to leave my children off to school, but I would go back to bed immediately afterwards. Over the days, weeks, and months that followed, regardless of what I read, I wasn't getting any relief.

That is, until one day.

* * *

As usual, I was lying on my bed and the children were at school. I found myself surrounded by books. These were generally on the subjects of bereavement, depression, mental health and, of course, suicide. On that morning, however, for some reason I picked up a book that was not about any of those topics. This book mainly dealt with art through the centuries. It featured the greats, like Picasso and da Vinci. It revealed such remarkable paintings and sculptures – art that would make you stop in your tracks and wonder how anything as perfect as this could come from the hand of a human being.

There was one artist in particular whom I will never forget: Michelangelo. This young man, at just twenty-three years of age, had carved a sculpture out of one very large piece of marble. His main model of inspiration was a woman called Mary of Nazareth. This humble, ordinary woman became the main focus of the sculpture, the *Pietà*. Housed in the Sistine Chapel in Rome, the *Pietà* shows Mary, a mother, cradling the dead, broken body of her crucified son. His lifeless body is sprawled across her lap, while she looks intently into his face.

While this image of love is something that could be recognised by any parent, whether their son died in a war or through an accident, whether through a terminal illness or through suicide, it was not this that grabbed my attention. It was the symbolism of the sculpture. Michelangelo based these two people on a man and woman who lived thousands of years ago. He would have known that the physiques of men and women who lived all those years ago would have been very different. Back then, women were very small in stature, usually no taller than five feet in height, but Michelangelo's Mary would have been eleven feet tall standing upright. Her body was so strong, her lap so deep, it was obvious that she was capable of holding and cradling the dead body of her large-framed, adult son, Jesus.

This incredible sculpture held something truly magical for me – staring at the mother's expression was an epiphany for me. It was the look of incredibly tender, compassionate acceptance written on her face that made me sit upright and realise that this is what our country needed. We needed a *Pietà* in every community so that we, too, could look on people who were in distress with tenderness and compassionate understanding.

I remember that day as if it were yesterday. It was a light-bulb moment that made me jump out of bed. With this 'look' of compassion still in my head, I ran down to Lucan village to Kieran Brady's office. Kieran is an auctioneer whom I knew, admired and trusted. I told him I wanted to buy a house. What I had in mind was a house where the person in crisis would be embraced and held until they could walk on their own again. A professional service that would provide a new therapeutic model, which would view people as people in short-term crisis rather than people who needed medical intervention.

After listening intently to me, he said with great wisdom, 'Joan, what you want is to create a charity.'

After my conversation with Kieran, I spoke to my brother John Lowe (who later became known as the Money Doctor). They both convinced me to start a charity, an organisation that would help people in suicidal crisis, openly, compassionately and with incredible acceptance. In January 2006 Pieta House opened its doors. That was the genesis of the charity in a nutshell, but actually, it was a little more involved than that. I started by lobbying the HSE for a vacant building, and when this didn't succeed, I decided that I'd simply have to buy a house myself. By some miracle, a benefactor appeared who paid for the deposit and the first year's mortgage on a suitable house in Lucan, but we were still short of funds to get the service up and running. So, I went home and explained to Pat that we'd need to raise the remaining £130,000 by remortgaging our house. I can't imagine anyone else would have agreed, but Pat did! It never even occurred to me that we might fail – it was simply not an option.

I learned a lot during the early years of the organisation. When Pieta House opened, we were constantly bombarded with statements like, 'Suicide is a selfish act', or, 'They are in a better place.' Let's be clear here: after many years of listening to people who attempted suicide but lived to tell the tale, we discovered that the majority of people who want to take their lives truly believe that their family would be better off without them. We discovered that a third of people who did go on to take their lives left letters trying to explain to their families why they were taking what they thought was the only way out. We found through our research that the word 'love' is often used in people's final letters. People often say, in good faith, that those who die by suicide 'are in a better place'. This expression is very telling. What are we saying as a society? That a person who may be suffering from mental distress is better off dead? Of course, family and friends know different. I would like to think that the opening of Pieta House also opened the minds of society.

In those early years of the charity, old beliefs were questioned because suicide was now being talked about openly. People, especially the older population, suddenly began to talk and share something they hadn't discussed before – that they had lost someone to suicide. I remember distinctly one woman telling me that her brother had drowned in the canal near her house. All through the years the family had spoken about it as an accident, that he fell in, lost his footing. She knew the truth: her brother died by suicide. This woman was a nun. It was the first time in forty years that she had spoken about the terrible tragedy.

Pieta House was opened after much thought and organisation. I carefully selected people whom I knew would rally round and believe in the cause. Cindy O'Connor, who eventually became one of the most respected authorities on suicide, joined me the first day we opened. Barbara Coughlan, who was the biggest advocate and fiercest protector of the organisation, also joined that day, and eventually so did Celine O'Carroll, who became responsible immediately for all things financial. Of course, my own family were there to support me: my daughter Marie who, at twenty-two, was the wise, gentle owl on my shoulder, whispering advice when I was too angry with grief to think straight. My husband, Pat, although not a member of staff for obvious ethical reasons, became a temporary board member until Pieta could fill in all the board roles, essential for proper ethical and accounting oversight. And last but not least, my sister Marian, who to this day is my personal interior designer and was an 'everything else designer' for Pieta House. Marian never looked for any recompense or thanks for years of bringing the 'look' to Pieta House. This would become the template of how a counselling centre should look and would be adopted by many organisations in later years. Until Pieta House, mental health services were offered in gloomy Victorian buildings, and were often cold and clinical spaces, with hard wooden chairs and linoleum on the floors. At Pieta House, we wanted people to feel that they were coming home, to comfortable couches, candles, warm carpets and tea and biscuits.

* * *

That is my beginning, and yet every new milestone for Pieta House became *the* beginning. Every person who wanted to take up the baton, or who wanted to take a service to their community, every person who was drowning in grief and wanted to atone for their loss – that was a new beginning. The following stories are from the people who made that new beginning – who made Pieta House and, indeed, Darkness into Light the incredible soothing and hopeful light it is today.

CHAPTER TWO

Maria

Serendipity, according to the Oxford English Dictionary, is 'the occurrence and development of events by chance in a happy or beneficial way'. I remember watching the 2001 American romantic comedy *Serendipity*, starring Kate Beckinsale and John Cusack, which tells the story of two people who are shopping in a jam-packed Bloomingdales at Christmas in New York; they both reach for the last pair of black cashmere gloves – and the rest is history. I remember thinking at the time that it was nonsensical mush! However, it was down to serendipity that Darkness into Light was created.

It's strange, the older I become, the more I realise that, while we may not always be aware of it, we are placed in situations, or even placed in front of people, for a reason. Although I believe that we are given choices about how to respond to any given situation or person, I sometimes wonder at the coincidence that brings us there. I look back at my life and realise that my choices, such as training as a counsellor, were not entirely random. Counselling led me to study psychology and working in a production company that made videos for tourists, where I had to speak directly to camera, made me fearless when I had to be interviewed by TV or radio. All these situations led to what I feel was my ultimate purpose in life: to start a suicide-crisis intervention service in 2006 and, thanks to serendipity, to come up with the idea of a walk from darkness into light. Throughout this book, you will see examples of serendipity but the most astonishing was the one that led to the beginning of this incredible movement.

It all started on a hectic day when I was trying to be in ten places at once. It was 2008 and Pieta House was, at this point, only a couple of years old and although I had the title of CEO, I was also the proverbial mother of all trades. In essence, I *was* the CEO, plus chief bottle-washer, fundraiser, HR manager, toilet cleaner and, more important than anything else, the first person to meet the client – and I loved it. The first Pieta House centre was situated in Lucan and when I was asked why I'd picked that area, the answer wasn't profound. I lived in Lucan and wanted to be able to walk to work. The funny thing is I never walked to work – I ran. I couldn't get there quick enough, because I felt a surge of energy at this new direction in my life and a sense of urgency about wanting to help others.

On this particular day, I was running down the long corridors in Dublin Airport to catch a flight to Cork. For those of you who would take the train, a flight might seem a bit self-indulgent, but at €45, the flight was saving time and money, both of which were in short supply in my life at the time. Little did I know what serendipity was about to deliver. I was racing to this plane to attend the launch of a book by one of Pieta House's therapists, Marguerite Kiely, and it was an event I absolutely did not want to miss. But I had to be back at the office in time for a board meeting later that day. On that flight, I met Maria. Serendipity.

Let me give you a little bit of the background.

In the first year of Pieta House, we opened with a staff of six people. As the months passed, it became obvious that we needed more therapists. This was due not only to the increase in demand but also because it was essential that our therapists work no more than twenty hours a week, to ensure that their own mental health was safeguarded. We became familiar with the term 'vicarious trauma', which is the indirect exposure to someone else's trauma. This is a very real problem and it can impact the therapist's own physical and psychological well-being. Furthermore, if there is too much exposure to trauma for too long, a therapist can suffer from compassion fatigue.

Marguerite Kiely was taken on as a therapist in the early months after the birth of the organisation. She brought a calm, compassionate tone to the workplace and as the years passed, she developed a passion for the children who would come to us in acute distress, some as young as five years of age. She had the ability to talk to them at their level; she had the empathy to understand everything from a child's perspective. Children, young and old, loved her. It's no wonder, because Marguerite had four children of her own, two girls and two boys. Her second son died at the age of two from a very rare form of cancer. The death of a child, regardless of how they died, leaves an imprint on the heart and soul of a parent. Their lives are never the same again and while people learn to live with the loss, it never goes away. I always feel that the pain of grieving for a child is similar to a finger pressing a bruise, the colour of the bruise acting as a constant reminder of suffering, just as your thoughts return endlessly to the death of the child.

Marguerite discovered that one way of helping herself to come to terms with her baby's death was to channel her experience and grief into a book, *Aaron's Legacy*, which was published in 2008, and was the reason why I was rushing to Cork that morning. I was honoured that she'd invited me and wouldn't have dreamed of not being there to share in the occasion. Of course, typically, Marguerite had decided that she wanted the royalties of the book to go directly to a charity. As she is from Cork and, like all Cork people, is fiercely loyal to her city, she chose a local organisation, one which deals specifically with families, Brú Columbanus. This organisation provides accommodation for families of the patients of the various Cork hospitals, free of charge. It has been described as a 'home away from home', accepting people who live at least fifty miles outside of Cork and saving them the daily commute to hospital.

So, there I was, running down the gangway towards the Aer Arann flight to Cork, searching for my boarding pass and juggling folders, my handbag and my mobile phone. I clambered on board, saying hello to the air steward, then turned right to find my seat on the small aeroplane. I pushed my handbag under the seat in front of me and settled down for the flight.

I remember distinctly seeing Maria for the first time. It wasn't difficult to spot her – we were the only two people on the flight. I was sitting in my seat on the otherwise-empty plane when, all of a sudden, a young woman appeared in the aisle right next to me. She was looking quizzically at the number above my head. Instantly, I was sure that I had made the mistake of sitting in the wrong place. I immediately apologised, asking her if I had taken her seat.

I remember the gentle, respectful look she gave me, the type of look that was genuine and instantly made you feel at ease. She made some remark about Aer Arann placing us together for some reason, even though there was plenty of room on the aircraft. She was happy to move elsewhere, she told me. Yet, for some reason, in that moment, I felt an urge to engage with her and asked her to stay, not to move to another seat; after all, we were the only people on the flight and it was only for forty minutes. Whether she wanted to or not, Maria graciously accepted my suggestion and sat down beside me.

Serendipity. Who would have thought that a random journey, on a random day, would bring two random women together in this way? Whether it was our neutral surroundings or the fact that we were thousands of feet up in the air, we found ourselves having a deep conversation, sharing our thoughts on life, our feelings and experiences. We described our careers and our personal lives, talking to each other as if we had known each other forever. Although there was at least a decade of an age gap between us – I am the older of the two – we discovered that we had so many interests in common. Our conversation covered every topic and, between us, we solved the problems of the world. It was a true connection, made in an instant. It was one of those rare situations in which it is easy to talk openly and honestly about different aspects of your life. Concerns and issues that you probably wouldn't share with anyone close to you trip off the tongue so easily with a stranger.

I told Maria about my family, my children and my vocation, running Pieta House. I often find that when I tell people about my job, it opens conversations about deep life issues. Maria spoke to me at length about her life, her marriage to her wonderful husband, the time that she had lived in New York, before returning to Dublin, where she now lived. She explained that she was on her way back to see her parents, who lived in Cork. She spoke lovingly about them and about her family, telling funny stories about family holidays and get-togethers. It was clear that she was at the heart of a loving network of relatives.

She told me about her career working for many corporates over the years in an executive position. She'd been very successful and yet she also became the go-to person when a crisis occurred in the organisation. She supported and befriended colleagues who were going through difficult times and she seemed to have a natural gift for communication and empathy. One day, her innate compassion was tested, she explained. It was a cold December evening in New York in 1996 and the packed ferry that she was travelling on had just left Manhattan to cross the Hudson River to Hoboken, New Jersey, where she lived at the time. It had been a busy day at work and Maria was looking forward to a quiet evening at home. Then her phone rang.

It was truly devastating news. Her friend was calling from the other side of the country to tell her that her son had died by suicide. The shock numbed Maria to the core. He was just twenty-eight years old, a son, a brother, an uncle, a brother-in-law, a grandson, a nephew, a cousin, a friend, a musician, a poet and a businessman. To make it even more difficult, one of his parents would have to travel to New York from their home thousands of miles away to identify his remains. Maria, of course, supported and carried the parents during the difficult days that followed.

Maria's experiences offering support to family, friends and colleagues led her eventually to begin another journey, this one fortuitous. She began to run to raise funds for various charities, eventually competing in marathons all over the United States: Alaska, Boston, Washington DC, San Diego, San Francisco and many other places. Then she branched out beyond the States to run in marathons all over the world, including in Ireland. In fact, Maria had run nine marathons across the globe – all to raise money for different causes, ranging from breast cancer to Alzheimer's. She was driven by the understanding that the charities she ran for depended heavily on fundraising events, something with which I was familiar, but she was also spurred on by the incredible encouragement she got from friends and family and from the corporate world, who would show their trust and backing of her through their sponsorship. Maria raised thousands of dollars for her chosen charities.

She told me this humbly and matter-of-factly, not seeking praise, but simply sharing her experience with me. As it happened, I was going to take part in the Dublin Marathon that year and so was Maria. It would be my first marathon. I was hoping for support from friends and family, and sponsorship from the corporate world. In my innocence, I thought that if I completed the marathon, I would raise €250,000, which would have secured Pieta House financially for six months at least. I raised €250 – and most of that was from Pat, my husband. I should have raised €250,000 for the agony and torture of walking over 26 miles alone! Yes, I was walking the route, not running it, and I can still remember thinking that the idea of trying to complete a marathon in one day was inhuman. It ended up taking me over seven hours to complete. I suffered with shin splints on and off throughout the walk and then when I reached the 18-mile point, I hit a brick wall. The one thing that kept me going was the knowledge that I was going to treat myself to a chip butty at the end, paired with a glass of wine.

My friend and walking buddy Dolores sailed through the course with ease, while I huffed and puffed and struggled, finally crossing the finish line, utterly exhausted. Of course, Pat was waiting for me and had the car parked as near as possible to the finish line, because there was no way I was going to walk another step if I could get away with it.

At the finish line, although I gave Dolores a congratulatory hug, I did not feel any jubilation: I was traumatised. I just wanted to stop moving and to go home and have that chip butty. We stopped at the shops on the way home because I knew we had no bread, but neither did the shop. The chipper wasn't open either – of course it wasn't, it was a bank holiday Monday. I swore I would never do a marathon again, and yet Dolores was only delighted to participate the following year. Each year since, during the October bank holiday weekend, I watch the marathon from the comfort of my chair and I often think of Maria and how she accomplished so much with all her marathons. She was driven by the needs of others, while I was driven by a chip butty!

When we discovered that we had marathons in common, even though her achievements far outranked mine, I asked

Maria if she had a favourite country or event. She answered immediately, telling me of a walk that took place in Washington DC. It was different to any other marathon in that, firstly, there was a fee of $1,000 to register and, secondly, the run took place during the night. All the money that was raised went to a charity that dealt with suicide awareness. I was fascinated. I bombarded her with a million questions: what sort of person would have participated? What was the route like? What time did it start at and what time did it end? Did she run the whole route or walk some of it? Maria answered each of my questions patiently, explaining that the run commenced at 9 p.m., just as it became dark, and finished approximately five hours later in the depths of the night. This event was definitely for runners only and excluded walkers and people who would like to have been involved in the experience but could not afford the steep entry fee.

It was another light-bulb moment for me. Could an event like this work for Pieta House? My mind started whirring. I was moved by the idea that the run took place in the dark. It seemed to me to represent the place in which people find themselves when they are suicidal; however, there needed to be some light at the end, I thought to myself, there needed to be hope, a knowledge that suicide could be prevented. I also thought that running 26 miles was crazy because you were immediately cancelling out a massive cohort of people who would not physically be capable of taking part.

I thought that, firstly, if we were to have a walk, our registration fee would have to be minimal and we would also have to allow for those who could not pay at all; and, secondly, we'd be ruling out a large slice of the population if we made the event a run, whether it was 26 miles or 2 miles. It needed to be a walk, it needed to include people of every age and ability and I wanted it to speak about the message of Pieta House. While the

Washington marathon was deeply symbolic, it seemed that its central message was to raise funds for charity. There is nothing wrong with that. The purpose of events such as these is to raise much-needed monies to sustain a charity, but I wanted it to be about more than raising funds. If we were to have an experience like this in Ireland, I wanted it to tie in with the purpose of Pieta House – to bring people out of the darkness into the light.

I remember turning to Maria and asking her if she thought it would be possible for me to bring a similar event to Ireland. I will never forget her response: she said that of course it would be possible and whispered to me, 'Go for it.' I got off the plane elated. I had a new sense of purpose: a fundraising, awareness-raising walk that would allow people of all shapes and sizes to commemorate loved ones or to simply offer support. I could feel the excitement of it rushing through me as I made my way to the bookshop for Marguerite's launch.

* * *

Once Maria and I had bonded, we kept in touch with intermittent phone calls, emails and cards over the next few years. In interviews, I would often refer to Maria (who was too modest to allow me to give her surname) as the inspiration for Darkness into Light. I know she watched with disbelief the growth and expansion of the walk we'd discussed that day in 2008 into a movement that surpassed anything we could have imagined. By sheer coincidence, we bumped into each other at the Dublin Marathon a few months after that plane trip. Out of all those thousands of participants, we were within feet of each other. Serendipity. Maria was with her sister and, of course, she was running not walking, so after greeting each other warmly, the two ladies sprinted off, leaving me in a cloud of dust. I walked purposefully, pretending that I, too, was a fit athlete.

Who would have thought that a brief conversation between two ordinary women would become so important a part of the life, indeed of the future, of Pieta House. Those forty minutes were responsible for planting the seeds of an idea that ended up becoming a reality, a movement that took Ireland by storm, eventually spreading the message of suicide awareness to the wider world. The Darkness into Light movement would raise funds for our services but, more importantly, it would give men, women and children across our nation and globally the opportunity to unite in the darkest hour before dawn to walk together towards the light. These people would fearlessly remove the stigma around suicide, but their journey would also bring hope to thousands of people, by showing all those who were alone in the dark that there is a future of compassion and hope.

And so it began.

CHAPTER THREE

Dolores

I peered out of the bedroom window. It was autumn and it had only started to get bright, but it was bright enough for me to see that it was drizzling. It was the sort of rain that would get into every crease and crevice, adding more hardship to the walk I already dreaded. I had to meet my training partner, Dolores, for our training session for the Dublin Marathon, which was now just weeks away. Our sessions always took place on Sundays and they were always at least five hours in length, which I found challenging, to say the least. Not to mention the fact that my fundraising efforts hadn't gone to plan, relying on the generosity of my husband and Jason, our cleaner in Pieta House, to raise a tiny fraction of my € 250,000 target.

Today, of all days, I didn't feel like going for a long trek. I was tired. I had landed back into Dublin the afternoon before, on the Aer Arann flight from Cork. I'd had to leg it into Lucan for our board meeting at 7 p.m. It was exhausting, but the board meeting was really important to all of us at Pieta House. I am always amazed at the generosity of people who volunteer to be board members. The meetings may only take place once a month, but the amount of back-office work that is needed, particularly from the chairperson, would make you believe that their only focus is that particular board meeting and nothing else. The people on the board of Pieta House were devoted to the organisation. Besides bringing along their individual talents and professionalism, they were the cheerleaders, proud and excited to be part of an organisation that was going to challenge social norms around suicide.

As I peered out the window, I was dying to tell Dolores about this wonderful young woman I'd met on the flight and the idea that she'd given me for a walk from darkness into light. If I could rely on anyone to listen to this idea, it would be Dolores. She had a practical, no-nonsense approach to life and its problems. After all, it was she who'd made me persist with the drudgery of training for a marathon. There was no way I could phone and ask her if we could skip the training – believe me, I'd tried! She'd merely answer: 'I'll see you at the usual place in ten minutes.' Now, I was really hoping that my back would act up or that I'd get sudden double pneumonia, before reckoning that even if I did, she'd have no sympathy. She'd have simply rocked up to my door and told me to get up and get out.

Although I had known Dolores for a long time, we hadn't become friends until I'd started Pieta House. Pat, my husband, had introduced me to her. He'd come to know her on his regular trips to Musgrave's Cash and Carry, as it was known then (now Musgrave MarketPlace) to buy supplies for his business. Dolores was a sales rep for the company and if I went along with Pat, we'd bump into her in the little coffee shop attached to the building. We immediately hit it off and, like two old biddies, we would start yapping away about anything. I admired her. She was glamorous, professional and very confident in her work. She would travel the country supporting existing shop owners and identifying new ones for the company.

Dolores introduced me to her partner, Matt, and over the years, we'd gone out a few times for a drink or a meal, even though we'd probably not see each other again for months. Both Matt and Dolores were extremely supportive of Pieta House right from the beginning, raising funds and being cheerleaders for the organisation. I remember they held a race night for us in the Red Cow Hotel on the Naas Road, where, thanks to Dolores and Matt, I met Tom Moran, owner of the hotel, who, many years later, would walk from his home town of Athea in west Limerick all the way to Dublin to raise funds for Pieta House.

My friendship with Dolores had grown over the years. Her steady, can-do attitude was exactly what I needed when work was challenging. Dolores would be the first person I would call if ever we lost a client in Pieta. Every staff member would be devastated, of course, and we would attend the wake and the funeral, but each time someone died, I always felt a piece of me had been broken, and Dolores understood this.

My experience walking the Dublin Marathon was unhappy but, thanks to Dolores, training, though certainly gruelling, proved to be therapeutic for me. We'd meet at the entrance to Lucan Demesne, a lovely park that runs down to the Liffey and was once the home of Patrick Sarsfield, hero of the siege of Limerick. Our route took us through the demesne to Leixlip, where we'd walk through the village and head towards Maynooth. Then we would turn around and walk all the way back, but this time we'd go through Lucan village to Clondalkin. By the time we hit Tallaght, we would turn for home once more. The route was about 25 kilometres and, of course, after completing it I would have loved to go to the nearest pub and have a massive cheese-and-onion sandwich, swallowed down with a hot whiskey. Dolores would have none of it!

What was great about the walks was that for five hours we had nothing to do but talk. We talked about everything, from our childhoods to our teenage years. We spoke about the loves in our lives, the trials and traumas of family life, as well as lighter things like make-up, diets and all the topics that people often share when they are together and know each other really well.

As our closeness grew, so did Dolores's loyalty and commitment to Pieta House. She became our very own Red, the character from the film *The Shawshank Redemption* who can get anyone anything at any time. She would annoy all her contacts for anything we needed, whether it was Christmas hampers or the all-important tea and coffee. It might sound trivial, but the humble hot cuppa was the mainstay of Pieta House. Our first point of contact with a client was that moment when we'd offer them tea or coffee when they came in the door. New clients usually refused, but all the staff would quickly become the proverbial Mrs Doyle from *Father Ted*, 'Ah, go on, go on, go on.' So, of course, they would receive a cup of tea and a plate of biscuits whether they wanted it or not. Later, we found that most clients would arrive early for their appointment, enjoying the warm welcome, including the tea and biscuits, and the fuss the volunteers would make over them. If there was ever anything we needed, all we had to do was ring Dolores.

So, on this miserable morning, we hugged each other hello and she started telling me about a fabulous dinner she had cooked the night before and the people who came to her house to eat it. She is an amazing raconteur with an uncanny way of making the mundane sound fascinating. Anyway, I soon forgot the early hour and my moans and complaints in general. After we'd chatted for a while, I said, 'Let me tell you about my trip to Cork.'

Dolores was dying to find out. She knew Marguerite Kiely and that her book, *Aaron's Legacy*, was being launched. 'You know, it was a bittersweet occasion,' I said. Acknowledging Aaron and the terrible disease that took him at such an early age was heartbreaking, and yet, there was joy too. Marguerite had told the gathering that writing down her experiences, telling people that losing a child is the worst thing that can ever happen to a parent but that they could survive it, had been cathartic. She saw it as her mission to write the book about her and her family's experiences to help other people. She'd been so grateful that I'd made the journey, and so was I. I was honoured to have been invited and to have been present.

'But wait until I tell you about the woman I met on the flight to Cork,' I said to Dolores. The journey back to Dublin had been so different from the outgoing one: the plane was quite full, mainly with business people anxious to get home for the weekend. It was an unexceptional flight, everyone away with their own thoughts, which made the flight with Maria all the more important to me. 'Firstly,' I said, 'there were only two of us on the plane and the other person was a young woman, who turned out to be so interesting and entertaining.'

'In what way?' Dolores asked.

'Well, her name was Maria and she was on her way to Cork to spend a few days with her family. Just like the two of us, we started talking about everything under the sun and, of course, Pieta came into the conversation. At that point, I noticed that Maria began to listen intently. She asked questions and we spoke about how this service was needed in every county in Ireland.'

Dolores interjected, 'Don't tell me – she wants to bring Pieta to Cork?'

I shook my head, 'No, it was something far more unexpected than that.'

I told Dolores about the coincidence of Maria doing the Dublin Marathon. 'She won't be doing it like us, though,' I laughed, 'dragging our heels.' I told Dolores that Maria had completed nine marathons. 'But now to the most important part of the conversation,' I said excitedly. I told Dolores that Maria and I had talked about all the marathons that she had taken part in around the world. 'God, if only we were younger,' I added. 'We could do a marathon every year in a different country.'

Dolores laughed out loud! 'You *are* joking? Sure, it's almost impossible to get you to do a couple of hours training in Ireland – let alone anywhere else. What if there was a Spanish marathon – you wouldn't last two feet!' I forgot to mention that Dolores could be very mean at times.

'Well,' I continued, 'the most important thing is Maria said that there was a marathon in Washington that was her very favourite.'

'Why was that?' Dolores was all ears.

'Well, it started in the evening and the runners ran through the night, and they had to pay $1,000 to do it. But the interesting thing is this,' I continued, 'it was for suicide awareness. Can't you see the symbolism here? People in the dark, which symbolises depression, walking towards the light?' I paused. 'I then asked Maria if she thought we could do something similar in Ireland. And guess what she said?'

'What?' Dolores replied, looking at me intently.

'She said, "Why not?"'

'Why not,' Dolores repeated thoughtfully.

'I couldn't stop thinking about it on the flight home.' I explained to Dolores that having an all-night run could be dangerous, a marathon was too long and, also, by making it just a run, we would be eliminating thousands of people who might want to walk. We also couldn't charge €1,000 per person, because nobody would turn up. I went on, thinking on my feet, explaining that while raising money for Pieta was crucial, I felt that it was more important to create awareness of the service, and to work towards changing the Irish people's mindset around suicide. The only way to do this was to have an event that every man, woman and child could participate in. After my speech, I looked at Dolores and asked, 'What do you think'?

Dolores replied immediately, 'Well, go and do it then.'

I hadn't told her the really important bit yet. 'Okay,' I said, 'but on one condition – I want you to be the chairperson of the organising committee. I could have a committee ready for you in a few days. What do you think?'

Without blinking an eye Dolores looked at me and said, 'Yes.'

* * *

What was to follow was the beginning of a thirteen-year journey. Dolores often tells me that she can't seem to remember what life was like before she got involved with what would become Darkness into Light. Now, the first five months of every year are a blur of committee meetings, going on the begging trail to see what we can get for nothing and ensuring the safety of the walkers at the various venues. As she says, 'Every year I swear this is the last time I am going to be involved and each year, of course, I'm back at it, doing it all over again!'

Every year, she's drawn back by the stories she hears from absolute strangers, who tell her about their loss, their experiences. That is what the whole event is about: people's stories. As she tells me, 'Even though I might have known someone for a long time – I might have met them on my travels or for work – I might not know they had lost someone to suicide until they'd share their grief with me. It was as if I gave them permission to tell their sad story.' That's very true. Each year, Dolores and I are drawn back because of the stories, but also because of people's extraordinary generosity. Darkness into Light has a domino effect: it starts with one small gesture and turns into a never-ending avalanche of kindness.

* * *

I knew that before Darkness into Light Dolores hadn't been involved with any charity to the same extent. Neither had I, before founding Pieta House. Like most of us, she'd bought raffle tickets for the usual Christmas or Easter hampers, finding it easier to donate than to be involved. As she says candidly, 'I would rather put my hand into my own pocket than ask someone to donate. I have no idea how I suddenly developed such a thick skin because now I have no problem asking anybody for anything.' She credits the work that Pieta House does. 'There is part of me that believes that it could be down to the cause. Because it's for a suicide charity, that pushes and drives me into doing all that I can for it.'

Dolores grew up with four sisters, whom she calls four instant best friends. She had a happy childhood, going to school, playing skipping in the evening – everything that a normal childhood provides. She grew up, got married, lived in Australia for a while, had two children and worked for Musgrave's; however, like so many people, she would be touched by suicide, as she told me. 'I think it was at around the time that my son was fifteen years old, a tragedy occurred that is still as fresh today as it was when it happened thirty years ago. My son was good friends with the son of my own best friend, by a happy coincidence. One day out of the blue, this young boy took his life. He was fifteen too. I remember going to the child's funeral; the church was packed to the rafters. Everyone was bewildered. We were afraid to dwell on it. What if we thought about it for too long? What if it was contagious, what if it happened to another child?'

Her fears were real. In my experience, many people, young and old, can be influenced by the suicide of someone who is in their family circle or in their community. In a young person's case, it might be that they witness the attention that the child who died has received from the school and the community at their funeral and they wonder if they would receive the same amount of attention. In older people, copycat suicides can occur, sometimes as the result of abnormal or prolonged grief, especially when the person who died was a significant relative. In a community, someone might think, 'If this person, who seemed to have everything, took their life, what is the point of my life?'

Dolores was so right when she spoke about her friend's son. It is so difficult to hear the news that someone has died by suicide – but it's unfathomable when it is a child. 'My friend was inconsolable. Every time I saw her, she would say the same thing: "Why?" Thirty years later, she is still asking the same question, still haunted over the fact that there may never be an answer. I think I must have unconsciously absorbed my friend's incredible, sad yearning, because when I was asked to get involved with Pieta House, I didn't hesitate.'

I knew that picking Dolores as chairperson of a potential walk from darkness into light was one of my best ideas. She was ideally prepared for the challenge because of her job, which involved meeting people from all walks of life, and because of her outgoing personality. 'It was as if I was supposed to have done that type of work, met those people, because when I was asked to be chairperson, I know I was completely prepared. When I think back on the day when I was out walking with Joan, listening to her describing the young woman she met on the flight and the idea for a walk, little did I know that Darkness into Light would become a day of shared grief, but also of hope. Little did I know the magnitude and reach it would have in the world.'

I knew that I could rely on Dolores, but when she said yes, it was wonderful to see that it had a knock-on effect on everyone she met. Once they realised what the charity was about, they quickly agreed to help, because, as Dolores says, 'Everyone knows someone who has been touched by suicide. It wasn't just me who had absorbed someone else's sadness, the whole nation had absorbed it. You didn't have to go personally through the loss of someone to suicide to know what it would feel like. We all seem to have an innate sense of understanding how tragic and unspeakable it is to lose someone this way.'

* * *

Meanwhile, I had promised Dolores that I would have an organising committee for the inaugural Darkness into Light walk ready for her within a week. I just about made it.

The first meeting took place on a warm September evening. 'People spoke about it being an Indian summer,' Dolores recalls, 'as I made my way down to Pieta House. I brought my daughter Sinéad with me, not only for moral support but also because she is an IT legend and I knew her skills would be needed.' I opened the door to them both, telling them that they were the first to arrive. We all sipped tea, waiting for the doorbell to ring again. Within minutes, people began to arrive. While we were being introduced, I could see Dolores looking nervously around the table, not knowing anyone except me and Sinéad. We were something of a mixed bag – only one man, the rest women. We were all strangers, but what we all had in common was a desire to make this project work.

The one man was called Johnny and he'd come along with his wife, Gertie. They were new to the world of committees, but Johnny's experience in youth training would be invaluable, I knew. Although they were uncomfortable at first, I had confidence that they'd soon get the hang of it, and that this project would be good for them. Next to them were two younger women, Suzanne Graham and Avril Copeland. They both appeared confident and knowledgeable. Next to Sinéad was a slight woman, Cathy Kelly, who also appeared confident, in spite of the fact that, as we found out later, she had no idea why she was at the meeting and was there by default. Thankfully, Cathy would more than prove herself by being by far the most organised person out of the lot of us, as Dolores reminds me.

I gave a brief description of the work of Pieta House and outlined the project I had in mind, then said, 'And now, over to our chairperson, Dolores.' I'm sure that she wanted to bolt from the room at that point.

'I nearly backed out. These people thought I knew what I was doing. I wanted to laugh,' Dolores tells me, adding that she has absolutely no recollection of the content of that meeting. Yet, somehow we all managed to come up with a plan for that first walk, which would take place at 4 a.m. in the Phoenix Park in May 2009. Somehow, this group seemed to fall into an easy partnership and we would spend the next twelve years coming together every week, beginning just after Christmas, to work out how to make each year's walk more successful than the previous year's.

'It was incredible,' Dolores says. 'Each one of us brought a gift or a talent to the table. Johnny with his experience with marathons and running clubs. Avril because of her experience of taking part in triathlons. Suzanne was a chaplain at the local secondary school, who had great knowledge about teenagers and would bring busloads of them to the walk over the following years. Cathy, as it turned out, was co-director of a building company and had a wonderful business head. Gertie was quiet at the meeting, but afterwards confided that she was there to ensure that her reluctant husband would get involved, an important role in itself. This was the beginning – we were off.'

* * *

It was a very steep learning curve. There's a big difference between having a brainwave and being able to make it happen. We set the entrance fee at €20, which was felt to be affordable, and the venue of the Phoenix Park was decided on because there was an already-established 5-kilometre circuit there so all we had to do was use their template. It also had lots of parking and was central in the city. Also, as there was an established circuit, the Office of Public Works (OPW), which gives permission for this kind of event in public places, readily agreed.

On the morning of the first Darkness into Light, we came across a major unanticipated stumbling block: it was pitch black and we could hardly see a thing. Dolores has a much clearer memory of the event, because of her sterling work on the committee: 'The first year of Darkness into Light gave us such insights into how to run an event like this. For a start, it was at four o'clock in the morning. It was pitch black and all we had with us were torches and one lamp that was fed off some sort of generator. We'd borrowed a small type of garden gazebo from Avril's parents. Suzanne had borrowed a loudspeaker from her school. God knows what she was shouting into it! In the following years, she would be the person at the finish line, shouting out her praise and encouragement to the people who had completed the walk. Johnny was trying to direct people to the start line, ably supported by Gertie, who, even though she wasn't physically able to take part, was her husband's right-hand person.'

Cathy was helping people to register while I, apparently, was running around like a headless chicken. I had persuaded Pat to collect the entrance fees from people. He had no change with him and because it was so dark, he couldn't see anyway, so he kept stuffing notes into a large money bag. When we think of how amateurish we were – yet for some reason it worked. People emerged from the darkness and started coming towards us, attracted by the one light, asking if they were at the right place.'

Dolores reminds me that over 400 people turned up that night – one of them a friend of mine, Barbara Cantwell. She and her friend Iris drove to the Phoenix Park and could neither see nor hear anything. They were convinced they were at the wrong place. They were nearly going to give up when they saw a light and headed towards it. They had to make their way through bushes and long grass, and all of a sudden they heard a voice say, 'Howya.' It was Pat. Afterwards, Barbara told me that she and Iris had started out on the 5-kilometre walk questioning their own sanity for getting up at such a ridiculous hour, but then they started chatting and were so busy sorting out their own problems and the world's problems that they didn't even notice when the walk ended.

For me, looking back at that morning so many years later fills me with emotion. To be there, witnessing the power of people in action, to feel that I was seeing something extraordinary, was a moment I'll never forget. But it seems entirely appropriate to give the last word to Dolores, because without her months of work, the event I'd dreamed into being on that flight to Cork would never have happened. Her words say it so much better than mine: 'As the shafts of sunrise started to peek from behind the dark sky, I remember looking over at the Pope's Cross and could see the sky becoming brighter. I suddenly saw scores of people walking quietly in unison. I couldn't believe it! We did it! People had really gotten up and come out in the dark to walk for Pieta House. Now that it was full daylight, I could see the people more clearly. There was such a mix: couples holding hands, some crying as they came over the finish line, but also people who clearly wanted to do the journey on their own. I remember spotting an older lady, who was clutching a pair of rosary beads. She was obviously remembering someone who had died by suicide. She didn't need to explain; we all knew the reason why we were there. We felt an incredible sense of achievement but we also realised that we had just witnessed something magnificent.'

Suzanne Graham, Dolores Ronan, Avril Copeland and Sinéad Ronan-Wells,
original committee members

Johnny and Gertie Fox, original committee members

Joan Freeman, Tom Moran and Brian Cody

Maeve and Alan Gallagher who started
the Darkness into Light walk in
Westport, Co. Mayo

Marie and Denis O'Carroll
Inset: their son Nathan

Rebecca Skedd (right), CEO of Solace House, New York, with two of her colleagues for the first Darkness into Light walk in New York

Large group of walkers at the first Darkness into Light walk in New York

Members of the original Darkness into Light committee winning
Best Charity Event at the Irish Fundraising Awards 2012
(back row) Suzanne Graham, Avril Copeland, Sinéad Ronan-Wells, Johnny Fox,
and Richard Dixon, chair of the judging panel;
(front row) Mary Kennedy, Gertie Fox and Dolores Ronan

Suzanne Graham, Avril Copeland and Sinéad Ronan-Wells

CHAPTER FOUR

Johnny and Gertie

The assessment room in Pieta House doubles up as a boardroom. This large room has an impressive fireplace, flanked by two comfortable sofas. A long mahogany table is situated at the end of the room, its highly polished top reflecting the chairs that surround it. Candleholders and soft pictures are dotted around, the tea lights always lit when a new client is expected. The room is warm and welcoming, nothing like you would expect of a mental health service. But the object that stands out most in the room is a sturdy little pouffe that is placed strategically in front of the couch. That's where I would usually sit when talking to new arrivals.

It is the most important seat in the building because it places the therapist within inches of the distressed person. For the first few years of Pieta House, I was the assessor, which meant that I took the initial assessment of the person's needs and situation before allocating them to a therapist. I had the immense privilege of meeting the new clients, welcoming them into this lovely room and hearing their stories. The clients would inevitably cry and I would find that I had to reach out and touch them, to hold their hand or rub their arm. I couldn't bear to just sit there, unflinching, while they wept in their sorrow.

Although this assessment was just the start of the therapeutic process, it was the most important part. This is when the distressed person would decide whether they wanted to come to

Pieta House, where we would help them to discover why they were here. After hearing their story, the first question I would ask is, 'Why do you want to die?' This was followed by, 'And why do you want to live?'

The room was my favourite in the house. Although it was filled with many sorrowful stories, it was also filled with memories of comfort, understanding and compassion. It was a room where people were listened to without judgement, where they were accompanied on their difficult journey by someone who would catch them if they were to stumble.

It was into this room that I led Johnny and Gertie Fox in August 2008, not knowing exactly what I was going to hear.

I had received a phone call from a social worker attached to a convalescent home in Dublin. The conversation was brief: she asked me if I would talk to a couple that she'd met when the woman, Gertie, was a patient there, about a recent loss. They did not want counselling, she told me, indeed, they had to be persuaded to come to see me, but she thought that a chat at least would help. The man, whose name was Johnny, would come only because Gertie had said to him that it would be rude not to, after the social worker had gone to the trouble of contacting me.

I remember the afternoon well, a mild autumn day. The room looked particularly welcoming because one wall had just received a coat of paint that was a shade of fresh-apple green. I had advised the receptionist that when the doorbell rang, I would answer it as I wanted to bring the couple straight into the boardroom.

Right on time, the doorbell gave a short ring. I hurried out, smiling as I opened the door. My smile froze when I saw the couple in front of me. Gertie looked as if she would blow away in a puff of wind. Her gaunt, grey face and hollow cheeks showed the trauma she was experiencing. Knowing that she had just come out of a convalescent home, I helped her up the step as she leaned heavily on sticks that she held tightly in her thin, bony hands. She looked at me and said nothing, but just nodded her greeting.

Gertie was followed by Johnny. He hovered behind her, directing her into her chair. He, too, glanced at me, not wanting to make full eye contact. He was stiff with grief and his body language screamed that he did not want to be there. His face held a frozen look of sorrow. He also didn't speak at first: all you could hear from him were long, deep sighs that seemed to be coming from his soul.

I offered them tea or coffee but both refused with the shake of a head. Gertie still did not look at me. Instead, her soft brown eyes looked briefly around the room and then dropped to look at her hands.

I said that I knew little about them, just that Gertie was recovering from an operation and that they had recently experienced a loss. I looked at them expectantly, asking them if they would allow me to hear their story.

There was silence. At first, I thought no one would speak. Both of them were still looking at their hands. Then Gertie said, 'Go on, Johnny – you tell her.'

Johnny lifted his face and for the first time looked me directly in the eye. 'Listen, love, no offence, but no matter what you say to us, it will not help us.' His tone was curt; he sounded angry. Of course he was angry, I thought. Not only was he having to deal with grief, but he was in a place that he did not want to be.

I nodded in agreement. I could imagine what he was talking about. Neither of them needed platitudes, or soft, meaningless clichés. What they needed was the truth. 'Look, I know that no words will help you or Gertie,' I began. 'You are both on a terrible journey that's only just started. But would you please tell me your story?'

There was a long silence while both of them considered my words, before they both nodded and Johnny began.

* * *

Like so many people who crossed the threshold of Pieta House, they had once lived a very normal life. Gertie and Johnny had been married for forty years and had twelve children, most of whom were living not too far away. It was a very busy household. There was always someone popping in, their children and then, later, grandchildren. Gertie was the matriarch, directing her children and her husband on a daily basis. Johnny smiled gently when he said this.

He himself had been a marathon runner, winning races on several occasions, and his photograph had even appeared in the *Evening Herald*. When he didn't want to run marathons any more, he joined local running clubs, not to run himself but to mentor and encourage children to do track and field. He was known by nearly all the kids in his neighbourhood in Tallaght, who respected and looked up to him. He would be at every fixture, shouting and cheering them on. He even had a couple of kids who did very well when they were older and who had run for Ireland. I became intrigued with the picture he was painting of this gentle couple.

Throughout the years, during all the times that were difficult, challenging and painful, they were a constant support to one another. Now, as he recounted the story, every few minutes Johnny would look at his wife and gently touch her hand. Even in his extraordinary sorrow, it was clear that he was thinking of her.

Their son Robert had been sick for months by the time he got a final diagnosis, going backwards and forwards to the hospital for tests and sometimes staying as an inpatient. The doctors reassured him, first saying that it was a virus, then it was an ulcer and then it was something else. During this period, Gertie and Johnny would visit Robert every day.

As Johnny recounted to me that they would always remember the day they went in and found their son propped up against several pillows. He was in a ward with other men, but it happened to be quiet when they arrived.

'Well, son, how are you today?' asked Johnny. It was always the first thing that was said and, normally, Robert would say he was grand, but today was different.

Gertie took up the story, 'He grabbed my hand and looked into my face and said simply, "I have cancer." My heart stopped. I heard Johnny gasp. Robert went on and said, "Don't worry, they told me it was curable."'

Gertie continued. 'I looked at Johnny and looped my arm through his. I don't know who was propping who up, but it was reassuring. Here was another challenge in our lives and together we'd meet it. Even if it was cancer, we'd support Robert and help him to get well. Then two doctors walked in, but Robert gestured that it was alright for us to remain. One of them said, "Now, Robert, you can go home but I want you back in here first thing Monday morning to start chemotherapy." I couldn't believe what I was hearing. Chemotherapy was so serious.

'We then learned that Robert wasn't well enough for the chemo, because he had fluid on his lungs, so the doctor said, "Well, come in anyway on Monday morning and we will assess the situation." We brought Robert home, not knowing that it would be the last time he would ever come home alive.'

Johnny took up the story then, telling me that Robert returned to the hospital on the Monday but died suddenly on Monday night. He had received chemo, even though he still had fluid on his lungs, because of the seriousness of his condition, but it was too late. Their baby, their firstborn, was gone. 'The whole family gathered around his bedside at the hospital. You could hear the girls crying. The boys stood there in absolute disbelief, except for Fergal, our youngest. He was wringing his hands; he looked completely lost. In spite of their ten-year age gap, he and Robert would do everything together. When they were children, Fergal would follow Robert around like a happy puppy. Robert always had time for him, and as far as Fergal was concerned, Robert was not only his hero but also his best friend.'

The months that followed were a blur for them both. It was difficult to keep motivated, even to get out of the bed in the morning. It was Johnny who encouraged Gertie, he explained, because she was worried about Fergal. What's more, the gloom in the house was reflected in the outside world. The economic crisis had kicked in and people, especially builders, were losing their jobs. Fergal was one of them, a double blow to him after the death of Robert. He had moved in temporarily with his sister, Susan, and her husband. Gertie and Johnny were glad, Johnny told me, because at least he would have company. They also would visit him every day, distracting him, encouraging him to be active. Both his sister and her husband were out working during the day, but each evening, on the dot of 8 p.m., they would return home to the smell of cooking. Fergal would make himself useful by tidying the house and cooking for them.

Gertie was in a lot of physical pain. Her hip needed to be replaced, but she had yet to receive a date for the operation and she was in a lot of discomfort. It was hard for her to get up out of chairs and almost impossible to climb stairs.

Meanwhile, Johnny was having his own struggles. Ever since Robert's death, every week he had still turned up at Tallaght Athletic Club to coach, often reluctant to go home after practice, even when everyone else had left the building. It was an oasis for him: for a few short hours he could forget about the sorrow back home. He would be compelled to put on a cheery face when kids would run up to him looking for his advice. He couldn't let them see his sorrow.

His peers, who were also volunteers, became his on-site counsellors and often the focus of his intense anger. He tried to keep that anger away from Gertie – she, too, was grieving – but he knew that he was safe with his fellow coaches. The guys in the club would let Johnny talk. Sometimes he was talking so rapidly and angrily that spittle would form at the corners of his mouth. It wasn't Robert's death that angered him; it was the injustice after Robert's death that had created this inner rage. Although it was difficult to believe that his son was gone, he had slowly accepted his death; he had no choice. What he would not accept was the cold, dismissive attitude of the hospital administration team after Robert's passing. One day, he went to the hospital looking for his son's death certificate – something no parent wants to hold in their hands – and he could not believe when the authorities told him that they had no record of Robert ever being a patient there.

Johnny was stunned. Of course Robert had been a patient there. He had died from cancer with his whole family around him. Did the authorities think that he was making it up? Every day, Johnny returned, presenting himself at reception, demanding answers. The indifference on the hospital's part felt like someone saying his son didn't exist. Not only were they not recognising his death, but they refused to recognise his life. One time, they actually called the gardaí because he was becoming a nuisance to them. Finally, finally, after he had to repeat the story to yet another official, the man gently said, 'Show me the ward your son was on.' Johnny walked the route to the ward where his son had died, knowing that, after this, he would never have to walk it again. 'It was here,' Johnny said when they arrived at the door to the ward.

They found Robert's details. His son's file was on a desk in the nurses' station. Soon after, Johnny could feel his rage subside, the life and death of his son was acknowledged, and that overwhelming rage was replaced with a dull ache.

* * *

In the months that followed Robert's death, Johnny found himself watching Gertie and Fergal in turn. Experts have always said that when parents lose a child, their relationship will inevitably suffer. How can they support each other through their mutually shared grief? Everyone has a different way of grieving. 'It was as if someone broke our left legs – how would we stand up? It's simple, we'd lean towards each other,' Johnny told me. Gertie had always been his rock. She was steadfast, solid; she carried the family through many difficult times. But this time, after Robert's death, she seemed to be flailing. She had become frail, she was in a lot of pain with her hip and there was an anxiety about her, and Johnny knew it was not only about his welfare but about Fergal's. Johnny always thought she had a sixth sense, an ability to almost predict when there was something wrong with their children, and she knew that something was wrong with Fergal. She was right.

Gertie knew that Fergal was becoming more despondent – keeping house wasn't enough to keep him occupied. He was a young, healthy man. He needed a job and a purpose in life. Every day when they went over to him, it seemed harder to engage with him, harder to try to make him more cheerful.

Gertie knew there was something wrong. There was something gnawing at her. She looked over at Johnny one evening over a cup of tea and whispered, 'I'm afraid.'

'Of what?' he answered.

'I don't know – something doesn't feel right.' They both jumped when the phone rang shrilly in the hall. It was Susan, and she was hysterical. Gertie couldn't hear what she was saying, but then she heard Johnny shout down the phone, 'What, what is wrong with him?'

Gertie whispered to herself, 'I knew it – my baby is dead.'

* * *

The night that Fergal took his life, Johnny saw his wife break right before him. All light was gone from her beautiful eyes. She seemed to crumple. She was suffering from an intolerable inner pain. She was a shattered shell of the person she'd once been. Johnny knew that his job was to carry her over the following weeks. They leaned on each other for support, but the weeks that followed were unbearable.

Johnny didn't return to the athletics club after Fergal's death.

A few weeks after they'd buried Fergal, a date arrived for Gertie to have her hip-replacement operation at the hospital. At first, Gertie refused to go. She had given up. 'What's the point?' she would say over and over. 'I'm not going anywhere, I will never leave this house, so what's the point?'

'She was refusing to get the operation,' Johnny explained to me as we sat together in the boardroom that day. 'She just couldn't see that life was worth living.'

It took all of Johnny's powers of persuasion to get Gertie to change her mind. When she went into the operating theatre, Johnny paced the corridor, waiting. When the nurse wheeled out her bed, he looked at his wife's tiny body and wept. He kissed her soft face and prayed that she would now at least get some relief from the months of excruciating physical agony. She had enough emotional agony to contend with.

Every day he would come into the hospital to be with her, but her recovery was extremely slow. The staff advised him that she would have to go into a convalescent home because she certainly was not ready to go home. They believed that psychologically Gertie was almost apathetic about making progress.

'I could feel myself beginning to slip,' Johnny confessed to me. Although Johnny continued to visit her every day, he was terrified that he was going to lose her and if he was honest with himself, he felt that he already had. If anything happened to her, he knew he would not survive. His sadness and despair seemed to be growing daily; in particular, when he would leave the convalescent home and had to face the lonely journey home. The house was empty without Gertie. He wouldn't, couldn't eat. His night was filled with dark dreams and his days were overrun by moments of fear. Any time the phone went, his heart would stop, thinking that something had happened to Gertie.

Gertie had been convalescing for a few weeks when Johnny was called into the office of the home's social worker. She told him that she was worried about his wife; she feared that if Gertie didn't get help with her grief, she would not recover. She was worried about Johnny, too. Would he consider seeing someone, a counsellor maybe?

Johnny shook his head, 'I don't believe in that mumbo jumbo.'

The social worker asked, 'How can you lift your wife when you are on the floor yourself?'

Johnny stood up to leave. 'We will be fine. We'll manage,' he said brusquely.

He left the office and went to the room Gertie was in. She smiled in greeting to him.

'How are you?' he enquired.

Without speaking, she handed him a card with a name and number on it.

'What's this?' he asked his wife.

'The social worker thinks we should go there.'

Johnny sighed in exasperation. 'No way are we going there. I don't want to,' he hissed.

Gertie took his hand and said gently, 'Well, I do.'

He gave in and looked at the card again. 'Who is this Joan Freeman anyway?'

* * *

For the next forty minutes all you could hear in the room was the voice of this broken man. Johnny spoke about his eldest son's suffering, of the last days of his life before cancer took him from them, and of his youngest son's bewilderment at the loss of his brother. While the whole family were distraught, it seemed that their youngest son had taken Robert's death the worst. He'd been heartbroken, depressed and had been robbed of the will to live. The pain was just too much for this young man, just as it was now for his parents.

When Johnny's tired voice quietened, all that could be heard was the sound of the soft, gentle sobs coming from all three of us. Although I have often cried in private after an assessment with a client, never before had I openly wept in front of two strangers. I was unable to speak; in fact, I could hardly control myself. I knew that I would be of no use or support to them if I was inconsolable. To allow myself some time to recover, I asked Johnny to tell me a little about their background and circumstances, while I tried to pull myself together. He had done so earlier, of course, but in the whirlwind of the trauma he'd then shared with me, I'd forgotten.

'Well, I used to be a runner,' Johnny began, somewhat reluctantly, going on to tell me about his marathon-running days, his involvement in athletics clubs and his contacts in the running world. He had incredible knowledge and his love for the children he coached was plain to see. How he must miss it, I thought.

Then I had a thought. If I couldn't persuade him to see a therapist, could I direct his grief into something more positive? I knew that there was very little chance that I would see either Johnny or Gertie again, so this might be my only opportunity to help them. Johnny had just the kind of insider knowledge needed for the committee that I had promised Dolores I would put together. I wanted to create a fundraising event that would be centred around a walk or run and here, right in front of me, was the most perfect expert in the area, with his support and strength beside him.

'Look, before we discuss counselling, could I ask you something?' I said to them both. 'I'm trying to put together a sponsored walk or run for Pieta House and I need an expert in the running area,' I began hopefully.

Johnny shook his head, 'Nah, nah, I'm finished with all that. I haven't been back in months. I don't have the heart or the interest.'

I could see that he was struggling again, tears welling up in his eyes. I took his hand gently and said to him, 'Earlier, you told me that no matter what I said to you, it would be no help. I know you are right, but I want *you* to help *me*.' I knew that all that sorrow and grief could be channelled into something that could help other families, something that could prevent other parents losing their children to suicide. 'You have talents that just need to be tapped into. You wouldn't just be helping me – but you could be helping hundreds of people. Will you help me?'

Johnny shook his head again. 'No,' he repeated.

'Look,' I said, 'don't say no now; just think about it.'

He shook his head for a third time, 'There's no point. I won't change my mind.'

I patted his hand and said, 'That's fine, but I'll give you my home number, just in case.'

We stood up at the same time and I told them that I'd be in touch very soon about allocating a therapist to them, still hoping that they'd agree to see one. Gertie struggled to get out of her chair, still fragile physically as well as mentally. I hugged her goodbye and then I hugged Johnny and walked them to the door. 'Thank you for coming to me,' I said.

Johnny remained silent and Gertie looked at me with a small smile, still not uttering one word.

A week later, Johnny and Gertie became the second and third members of the newly formed Darkness into Light committee.

CHAPTER FIVE

Learning on the Job

I suppose the best part of preparing this book and talking to people that I may not have spoken to in a long time was that it brought back many memories. As you can imagine, some were hilarious, some extremely tragic; but being in touch with each one of these incredible people, laughing and reminiscing about the early days of Darkness into Light, was a tonic. It was so lovely to share their recollections of their highs and their lows, their experiences of belonging to a group of people who were all trying to create an event, but also their own personal takes on the whole endeavour. Initially, their remit was to raise funds for Pieta House. It was only during and after the first walk in 2009 that they realised that there was something far more important here; more important than fundraising, more important than creating awareness.

Only as I am writing this do I realise that the most important part of the entire venture was acknowledgment. This walk was going to acknowledge that suicide exists. It was going to acknowledge the people who had already died by suicide – men, women and children who left an impact on the lives of the people around them. It was going to acknowledge that their lives were necessary, even if they didn't feel it themselves. It was then, of course, about acknowledging the sorrow and suffering of those who were left behind. There would be no more cover up, no more stigma around suicide.

I know none of us had any idea that we would change the social tapestry that existed in Ireland around suicide. If the committee had been given that as their remit, I doubt anyone would have stayed. I know I wouldn't have. There are many reasons why someone would join a committee or a board. It could be because they were asked, or because they had time on their hands, or it could be because it would look good on their CV (that's okay by the way). But this committee was different. Granted, a couple of people were nudged, but many of them had volunteered their expertise. Also, the core driving force in all of them was passion: they wanted the Pieta House service to work so that it could save lives. This was quite apparent even at the first meeting. Nobody was trying to outdo anyone else. They absorbed the information about suicide and self-harm like sponges, as if their lives depended on it. Each time they met, their passion was reinforced not by listening to me, but by a contagious energy that allowed them to believe that what they were doing was right.

After a while, the members of the committee settled into the job and each of them fell into natural roles. I attended the first few meetings, where I witnessed the unfolding of the characters of people I did not know. It was like reading a book: each chapter, or meeting, would reveal another aspect of the person and each chapter would cause me to admire and almost love them for their energy and commitment.

I have always loved people. I am a people-watcher. I would be quite happy sitting in a café or a bar in town looking out onto the street and watching people go by. I would make up stories about them – always dramatic ones. The chances are that none of them were leading the lives that I'd dreamt up and that were so vibrant in my mind. Still, I like to think that this interest in others helped me work with the many different people who came into my life during my time at Pieta House and with Darkness into Light.

The funny thing is, if you were to ask these people who they would choose to be on a committee with them, I doubt they would have chosen each other.

Take Sinéad Ronan, the only daughter of our chairperson Dolores. She was a young woman who had just returned from New York with her husband, delighted to be home after six years. As you can imagine, she would do anything for her mother after being away for so long. So, when Dolores asked her to come along to that first meeting about Darkness into Light, Sinéad felt she had no choice but to do the dutiful thing. Sinéad was a quiet, reserved person, who yet, when it was necessary, would have her say. In all the years I knew her, she never criticised anyone, just solemnly accepted them for who they were.

After that initial evening, she was hooked. Although she was in the presence of a mixed bunch of people, some of whom were in their thirties and others in their late seventies, she was able to connect with each one and over the coming years would often attend social events with them outside of the months leading up to Darkness into Light. At the beginning, Sinéad was responsible for the custom Darkness into Light t-shirts, which would be worn by every walker, and the production of which became one of the most stressful tasks to have. She remembers that she chose the colour yellow because it was the cheapest one you could get.

The very first year in the Phoenix Park, however, there were no Darkness into Light t-shirts, so the committee came up with the idea of awarding walkers a certificate of completion. They only printed a hundred, but for weeks afterwards people called the centre looking for their certificate of completion. The committee members began to realise the significance of the certificate and, in later years, the incredible importance of the t-shirts. Sinéad recalls that very quickly they became synonymous with the walk. The colour yellow, which she had picked by default, came to symbolise hope. It also became something of a uniform, with the Soldiers of the Dawn united for an hour in the war against suicide.

Even later, when the t-shirts had become available at pickup points around the city and then the country, they were an opportunity to connect. The committee organised these pickup points in shopping centres around the country and would give up their Saturdays to become event organisers and therapists rolled into one. They understood that for so many people these t-shirts were not memorabilia but a solid piece of evidence of the loss of a loved one and the suffering endured. There was one year, which each member of the committee remembers with absolute horror, when there was a serious delay in the delivery of the t-shirts. People were ringing Pieta House, distraught, looking for them in time to wear on the day. I do not use the word 'distraught' lightly, because this humble item of clothing was crucial to them. It represented a lasting memory of walking with thousands of souls who'd been through the same thing that would soothe them in the years to come.

The committee were the first to recognise and acknowledge that, while raising money was essential to maintain services, most people were walking for other reasons. This made the members more sensitive to the mood and the needs of the participants. One year, about seven or eight years after the initial walk, the management team in Pieta House suggested bringing in a professional event management company to run the walk. At this stage, the numbers had increased to the extent that the event was becoming a challenge to manage. It was believed that their expertise would make the event not only more professional, but also raise more funds. The idea was to digitise everything, with people registering and raising funds for the event online.

To incentivise people, they were given a flashing badge announcing how much they'd raised for Pieta House, presented after the walk. The central committee and also the regional ones weren't sure about his approach, because they felt it would take the walk away from its grassroots origin. Such issues are part and parcel of an event that outgrows its initial remit. It was a good problem to have, but it highlighted the gap between the two goals: raising funds and commemoration. The committee understood that for many of our older population, the internet, online pledging and websites could be daunting, formidable and, more importantly, exclusionary. It highlighted the fact that we should always listen to the people at ground level. Event management companies have their place, of course, but so does the heart and soul of an event like Darkness into Light.

These were the difficulties and challenges that Sinéad, as a volunteer, had to face. She never winced nor buckled, but she did cry when the flashing badges were kept in as part of that particular year's event. This wasn't because she'd lost an argument. It was because she understood deeply that for so many people the event wasn't about the money but the opportunity to remember loved ones in a positive way. The badges never appeared again.

* * *

Two other members of the committee, Suzanne Graham and Avril Copeland, were friends. As the chaplain of a local school, it was Suzanne who dragged Avril to the first meeting. I had met Suzanne a few times before that. In her role as both chaplain and teacher, she would come to us if she was concerned about one of her pupils; in fact, over the years she brought many children to the centre, sitting with them, comforting them, secure in the knowledge that they now had somewhere to go. I will always think of Suzanne as a ball of energy hurtling towards you: nothing was a problem; there was a solution to everything.

Underneath that energy and busyness, there was a tender, gentle heart full of loving-kindness.

It was Suzanne who came up with the idea of the Banner of Hope. She started off by borrowing a large white piece of cloth, which she pinned to a board and placed on a table next to the finish line. All it said in the middle of this homemade placard was 'Banner of Hope'. Markers were left beside it for people to write messages to their loved ones on it. I remember that Johnny and myself wrote a message each, thinking of someone in particular. The rest is history. Like the t-shirt, it became one of the most important parts of the event. Almost everyone who left a message mentioned 'love', almost all used the words 'missing you' and all wrote directly to the person who was gone. Without realising, Suzanne had created an important part of the journey for all the participants in the walk, one that was going to be replicated throughout the world.

In time, Gertie took on the role of looking after the Banner of Hope stand, sitting beside it, her gentle eyes encouraging people to write from their hearts and almost ensuring that somehow their loved one would receive it personally.

Suzanne was also responsible for setting up the numerous tents at the events (when we became more sophisticated), a makeshift stage, toilet facilities and managing the volunteers. I often thought over the years that if ever there were a natural disaster in this country, I would want Suzanne Graham to organise the response. It would be run with military precision and an iron fist, but with a heart that was moulded of butter.

Avril Copeland met Suzanne while the two were playing hockey. Avril complemented Suzanne's boundless energy with supreme resilience. She was an elite athlete and took part in extreme sports all over the world. She was powerfully strong, truly made of stern stuff, yet her face didn't reflect all that toughness. She had the eyes of Bambi, soulful, gentle, and a smile that would light up the room. Avril was the artiste of the group, commemorating the walk in photographs. She was a creative and incredibly talented photographer, even though photography was just a pastime. She had the ability to capture the emotion of each person she photographed during the Darkness into Light walks. While nearly everyone was smiling in them, there was poignancy about the photographs. You could tell the person's story just by looking at the photograph.

After taking hundreds of shots, Avril would select some and create a video around them, adding some background music that was moving and appropriate. Her video, which would be about three minutes in length, would be part of my presentation when I went around to groups and corporates to give talks. Most people would cry while watching it. No matter how often I saw these videos, I, too, would cry. Avril would also be in charge of the music for the morning of the walk, which would boom across the park. She would always choose an upbeat compilation that would inspire and at the same time energise, especially necessary for that hour of the morning.

When watching Avril at the meetings in the early weeks, I remember thinking that she had the ability to bring a steady calmness to the group. I never heard her raise her voice or complain, especially when the group found it hard to come to a joint decision. She would simply calmly give her point of view. I only saw her get cross once, and that was with me for not pulling my weight during the clean-up after the walk was over – she was right!

* * *

The biggest change was in Johnny. It was wonderful to watch the unfolding of an extraordinary character as this man came back to life over the weeks and months. Just two weeks before the first meeting, when I'd met him and Gertie in the boardroom, I'd seen a man who had given up on life, who was prepared to just exist in the aftermath of losing his two sons. At that first meeting, you could see that he was there under duress and I could imagine him going home after the meeting and telling Gertie that he would never go back to that place again. But he did come back and each time he came back, you could see the small spark of interest in his eyes grow.

At the third meeting, he volunteered some information and it was as if he'd parted the Red Sea as far as I was concerned. The committee had been talking about needing stewards for the walk, people who could stand and direct walkers on their way, highlight danger spots and the many other tasks that were required of a steward. Johnny suddenly piped up, 'I know where you can get any amount of stewards.' He volunteered to ask the athletics club for its help. Although he'd lost interest in his beloved club after the death of his sons, here he was now, suggesting that he talk to them about helping. This was another step in his recovery: he was going back to the club who'd supported and embraced him, a club that had given him years of joy, a place where he was needed. Now, here was the perfect excuse for him to return.

One evening, I was coming out of Pieta House after work when I met Johnny and Gertie at the door coming in for their meeting. I didn't recognise them. Gertie was walking using only one stick, her hair had just been styled and she had put on a little weight, which filled out her lovely face. Johnny was standing beside her, upright, purposeful and eager. What a fantastic word, 'eager', but that was exactly how he appeared.

'Where are you going?' I asked. I didn't remember them being on the schedule for counselling.

'We have a committee meeting, and if we're early, we get a cup of tea,' Gertie said. Ah, Mrs Doyle, I thought to myself, they were home. And Johnny was hooked on the work of the committee. He stayed true to his promise to get his hands-on stewards from Tallaght Athletic Club. He was responsible for them, training, advising and monitoring them and, when eventually there was more awareness, training them in health and safety, which also came under his remit. And where was Gertie? Standing right next to Johnny, his rock and his support, just as she'd always been.

* * *

If ever there was a problem when I was involved in Pieta House, I would always go to Cathy Kelly. She was a volunteer for the first couple of years and although she wasn't involved in the Darkness into Light committee from the beginning, she was certainly there after a few weeks. She was one of those dedicated, organised, committed human beings who give people the comfort of knowing that the job would be done and done well. Cathy kept notes from the very first meeting she attended right up to a couple of years ago when she moved on to work in another area of Pieta House. This record became her bible and she was able to refer to anything when necessary. Although Cathy was working full-time at her building company, she was her own boss, which meant that she could come to Pieta House and donate her skills and hours every Friday. I used to say that she put manners on us, in particular on the administrative side.

Later, when she agreed to work with Pieta House full-time, having been persuaded by me, she was the one responsible for installing an incredible software package that would enable us to manage our database. For the first time we were able to capture the information we would need for our research into suicide and for a whole lot of other areas that become necessary in a growing charity. Without affecting a client's confidentiality, we were able to glean important information about the problems with which they'd presented, as well as their age, gender and so on, and to follow up with the client after they had left the service at one month, three months and six months, giving us invaluable insights into the recovery process.

If the committee members needed anything, Cathy was the go-to person and people would often drop in on Fridays specifically looking for her help. As the years progressed, Cathy became the cornerstone of Pieta House and of the Darkness into Light walk, an intelligent, articulate and incredibly patient woman who brought us (kicking and screaming) from the dark ages into the modern world.

Holding all these elements together was Dolores. Her good humour and laid-back attitude was exactly what was needed to be chairperson of this group. She never got worried or upset about anything. She would calmly deal with any problems and if they were not solvable, she would simply shrug her shoulders and say, 'Sure let it be, I am not going to lose sleep over it.' But on top of all that, she was a professional and a brilliant salesperson. It was no wonder she became the top sales representative in Musgrave's: she could sell anything to anyone and then persuade them to give it back to her at no charge! Dolores also had the ability to let people be responsible for their tasks without looking over their shoulders, yet to know at all times what was going on. She also had a gift for bringing people together, encouraging them, supporting them and, at the same time, carrying them.

She must have seen many changes over the years in Pieta House, some of them not easy to accept, but she did so with a quiet dignity. Most important of all, she allowed me to leave this important walk in her hands. It never dawned on me that it wouldn't work. I don't think I ever asked her for a report of any description; in fact, she would often ask me for a report. A day or so before the walk, all I had to do was ask her what needed doing and she'd allocate me a task from her list. And she would tell me what to do.

* * *

At the beginning of Darkness into Light, there was only one committee: the Dublin committee, which, of course, was and is still made up entirely of volunteers, with Cathy being eventually replaced by Marie Peelo. Thanks to them, a template was created that would be replicated throughout all the participating towns and counties across Ireland. Whenever a new committee pops up around the country, they are supported and directed by a staff member of Pieta House, but they just have to follow the original template to organise their own walk.

When I think about the making of that original template, I realise we knew nothing! We had nothing to go on. Think of all the challenges that lay ahead for that very first committee. Just think about the enormity of the task. They had to choose a title for the event, the venue, the logistics of the route. They also had to look for volunteers. They designed the t-shirts, the posters, the registration cards. They came up with novel ideas, such as having gospel singers performing en route and, of course, the Banner of Hope. They also came up with all the other incredibly symbolic add-ons over the years; for example, the tea lights. Thinking back now, the trouble they went to, placing hundreds of tea lights into glass jars, not only for reasons of health and safety but also to stop the candles from being blown out. Then the wonder of little electric tea lights came along and saved this group endless hours of work. They spelled out the word 'hope', which became the core word for Darkness into Light.

For the first few years of the walk, this committee also supplied the ravenous participants with food and beverages, goody bags, hot dogs, cups of tea; in fact, anything that was donated to us. These were handed out after the finish line and family and friends of the committee manned all the stalls until, in later years, we were able to attract the scores of volunteers necessary.

In the first ten years, this group worked without the help of any outside agency. They were their very own experts. They were the marketeers, the designers, the public relations, the security, the music and video production artists and they were on hand to be therapist and friend to all the participants who needed that support. We often look back in absolute disbelief at what happened (and, to be honest, in terror of what might have happened) – all because of six ordinary strangers.

The new committees that were formed around the country would have their work cut out for them, no doubt; however, the format was there waiting for them. The hard work of designing and creating was already done. The blood, sweat and tears were already spent. The groping around in the dark, both physically and mentally, was complete. Soon the light of the Darkness into Light movement began to spread across the country with people in towns and villages all over Ireland organising their own walks. And when a town or village didn't have one, well, that could easily be rectified.

CHAPTER SIX

Nathan's Walk

It would be a mistake to describe the O'Carroll household as busy. That would be akin to calling the M50 a country road. Imagine the M50 on a Friday evening; everyone rushing home, cars bumper to bumper, noisy engines, blaring horns – and yet everyone makes it to their destination. That was the way it was with the O'Carroll family: father, Denis, working all the hours that God gave; mother, Marie, running a popular B & B in the tourist town of Killarney. On top of all that, five lovely and boisterous boys – Damien, Killian, Aaron, Ryan and Nathan – who would tear around the house rather than walk, would eat voracious amounts of food and yet always complain that they were starving; who would drop their worn (yet still clean) clothes, using their floor as a wardrobe, comfortable in the knowledge that they were loved by a father who was gentle and wise, and by a mother who was a softie. Each one of them could wrap her around his little finger; the youngest boy, Nathan, especially so.

People said that Nathan had the face of an angel, with his big eyes and mop of dark curly hair. Not only did he look younger than his fourteen years, but also there was an innocence and a sensitivity about him that were immediately endearing. Although his parents adored this part of him, they were not fooled by it and would often call him a little rogue.

It was coming up to Christmas, Nathan's favourite time of the year. He would look forward to it for weeks. He was the one in the O'Carroll home who was responsible for putting up the Christmas decorations around the house and adorning the tree. He would thoughtfully buy his mother scented candles smelling of cinnamon or fir trees, which would add to the atmosphere. Nathan's routine also consisted of watching seasonal films in the run up to Christmas Day, all of them with the same theme: the magic and wonder of that time of the year and, in particular, the miracle of Christmas. It didn't matter if he saw the same films each year; it was all part of the tradition.

This particular day in 2007 was no different, except that Nathan was off school. Even though he wasn't really sick, he had been finding it hard to go to school and was relieved and happy to be able to stay at home and watch his favourite Christmas films. That evening he and his mother watched *Jack Frost*, a sentimental film that depicts the death of a father and how his child copes with the loss. In the film, the tragedy is softened for the child when the father comes back as Jack Frost to be by his son's side.

The O'Carroll family had a night-time routine. Each night Marie would have her bath, then the boys would have their showers. This was so they could stay on in bed each morning for a few precious extra minutes. When the film was over, Marie trundled upstairs to have her bath and was followed by Nathan.

'Do I have to go to school tomorrow?' he asked with a cheeky smile.

'We'll see,' his mother answered.

Nathan headed towards his bedroom and Marie into the bathroom. Afterwards, she headed downstairs. This was the time of day she looked forward to most, because herself and Denis would have the sitting room to themselves and would talk about their day and what their plans were for the next day. That evening, the house seemed unnaturally quiet. Marie presumed that it was because Nathan's two brothers were already down for the night in their rooms, while her older son, Damien, was away in Cork.

When she walked into the sitting room, she noticed that Denis was slowly nodding off. She shook him gently. 'Where's Nathan? Did he not come down to say goodnight?' she asked.

'I presume he is in his bedroom,' Denis said.

Marie turned on her heel and headed back up the stairs. As she reached the top step, she knew that there was something wrong. She looked over towards her son's room and saw a shadow against the door frame, the shape of a young man. In that moment, she became instantly calm. She walked purposefully into Nathan's room and peered into his en-suite bathroom. He was dead. Even in death he was beautiful, his large eyes staring straight into hers.

Marie could have screamed, but instead, she quietly ran down the stairs to her husband. She was so conscious of her other two sons in the rooms beside their younger brother's. She did not want them to see Nathan like this. She spoke urgently to Denis, who immediately ran up to his son, while Marie ran to get a kitchen knife. Then they called the ambulance and waited. It was 10.30 p.m.

The weeks and months that followed Nathan's death were a blur to the O'Carroll family. Hundreds attended his funeral. The Killarney community was rocked by the tragedy. While people offered their sympathy, it was obvious to both Marie and Denis that they all were at a loss for what to say. The couple tried to be strong for their other children but would collapse in each other's arms when they were alone. They became each other's prop, each being strong when the other buckled under the weight of their suffering. Marie wanted to move out of their house: it was too painful to remain. Every time she climbed the stairs, it felt like a rerun of that terrible night before Christmas. They were fortunate that their B & B business was separate to their home, so the family moved into the other house, locking the door of the family home without glancing back.

Marie and Denis poured their grief into supporting their children and working even harder than before. They often spoke about Nathan; in particular, about the signs they felt he was leaving them in the early months after his death. These signs would comfort them. Marie would tell people about the night that Nathan died, when Damien, his older brother, was in bed in Cork and had no idea of what had taken place at home. He had settled down in bed, yet he couldn't sleep; it was as if someone was yanking the pillow from under his head. It was 10.30 p.m. His uncle would soon be on his way from Killarney to tell him that his brother was dead.

Other signs were seen by many people in Killarney, who reported a strong blue light coming from Nathan's room, yet there was no one in the house. Like many bereaved people, the entire family became very aware of the presence of butterflies, even during the cold weeks of January, their gentle fluttering visible everywhere they went. Marie, in particular, would be conscious of her child's presence. She was sure that on her daily visit to his grave, she could spot him hiding behind the trees, peeping out mischievously. Although this gave her enormous solace, she was bereft.

For the next three years, she refused to go anywhere or see anyone, and relied heavily on the comforting love of Denis. Every year, when he suggested that they move back into the family home, Marie would come up with an excuse. 'Next year,' she would say.

* * *

One night in 2011, when the doorbell rang at the O'Carroll's, Marie had no intention of answering it. She was not expecting any B & B guests, so she ignored the second peal coming loudly from the hall. All of a sudden, she could hear Denis talking to someone, 'Yes,' he said, 'come on in. Marie is in the sitting room.' He opened the door and ushered in a woman Marie had not seen in a while, Anne-Marie Galvin, a local auctioneer who had children around the same age as Denis and Marie's sons.

She stood up to greet the woman, who gently kissed her. 'Marie, I'm sorry for dropping in like this without giving you any notice, but I thought I might as well talk to you face to face, rather than ring you.'

Marie gestured for her to sit down, while Denis sat opposite.

Anne-Marie began telling the couple about Pieta House, a service in Dublin that helped people who were suicidal and that they had an annual 5-kilometre walk that took place at 4 a.m. and ended while the sun was rising. 'They want us to hold one in Killarney,' Anne-Marie finished.

Marie was confused. 'Who is "us"?' she said.

Anne-Marie smiled, 'Well, obviously me and a couple of members of my family, but I was wondering if you and Denis would help out?'

Marie shook her head. She had been asked in the years since Nathan died to be involved in several worthy causes, but she didn't have the heart or the energy. Anne-Marie continued talking, more to Denis at this point because it seemed that Marie had disengaged. There was tenseness in her petite frame and a cloud of sadness seemed to envelop her.

Finally, Anne-Marie stood up and said, 'Look, just think about it. The team organising it will be coming down from Dublin next Thursday. We will be meeting at the Brehon Hotel at 7.30 p.m.' She squeezed Marie's hand before Denis brought her to the door.

'No way, Denis,' Marie said, when the visitor had gone. 'I have enough to do without adding more stress to my life by organising fundraisers.'

Denis nodded. 'I know, I know,' he said reassuringly. 'But maybe it's time for us to do something. There was another suicide in the town last week. Maybe it's time that we try to do something about it?' At this time, suicide rates were higher in rural areas than in urban areas and there was still a huge stigma attached to it, making it more difficult for families to deal with, no matter how much support they received from friends and family.

Marie looked at him in surprise. 'Sure, what could we do? We are still struggling with our loss. I am not in the frame of mind to help anyone, when I can't even help myself.'

Denis answered her gently, 'Sometimes it helps people when they reach out and help others. What have we got to lose? Why don't we go to the meeting anyway and see what the Pieta House people have to say and what exactly they want?'

Marie stayed silent.

* * *

The Brehon looked majestic as the sun was beginning to set behind it. Marie was nervous. This was the first time she had ventured out socially since Nathan had died, more than three years before. Denis held her hand as they walked into the foyer, looking around expectantly, as they searched for a familiar face. They saw Anne-Marie sitting at the far end of the lounge. She was surrounded by six people. Denis and Marie knew four of them, but the other two were strangers.

Anne-Marie waved to the couple, smiling. 'I'm so glad you came,' she said. 'Let me introduce you to the people from Pieta House.' She gestured to the man and said, 'Denis, Marie, this is

Kieran Brady.' Kieran, our head of fundraising, shook hands warmly with the couple and they murmured their greetings. Anne-Marie went on and placed her hand on the arm of the woman standing next to Kieran, 'And this is Joan Freeman.'

* * *

This is where I came into the O'Carroll's lives. When they walked towards us that evening, in 2011, I noticed an air of sadness, almost defeat, about them – and yet, there was an incredible sense of unity between them. Denis was protectively clutching his wife's hand. Marie was a beautiful, petite woman with long dark hair that curled around her face. Her large brown eyes stared at me sceptically as she shook my hand.

Our group was shown to a table for dinner but, as it turned out, Marie and I didn't eat one bite of food. I sat next to her deliberately, and instantly we warmed to each other as we began to talk. The volume of our conversation was low. We were oblivious to everyone around the table talking noisily. Every now and then I would see Denis glance over to Marie and myself, watching her, on alert, ready to shield her and to fight for her. There was no need.

I began to tell Marie about the service in Dublin, why it was started, the pain and sorrow that would come through our door in Pieta. She listened intently. Then she began to talk. I heard about Nathan. Every time she mentioned his name, her face would light up but her expression would quickly be replaced by a sorrow that was palpable. She told me that she'd found her boy hanging in the shower and how, protective of their children, she and Denis had quietly cut their son down and laid him on the bed. She had known instinctively that if she had screamed when she found Nathan first, his brothers would have run out of their rooms to see what was wrong. They would have seen Nathan and would have been left with an image that no person, in particular children, should ever have to remember.

As she continued to speak, I realised that my first impression of her as a defeated, grief-stricken woman was completely wrong. Here was a lioness, a woman whose first priority was to think of her children and to continue to support her husband; however, the lioness was wounded. We spent the next few hours talking, listening, crying and even sometimes laughing. Marie told me about all the signs that she and her family would experience that let her know that Nathan was close, especially the butterflies. She recalled the white butterfly that had rested on Nathan's coffin in the church on the day of his funeral; and how as they'd climbed into the car on their way to the church, Denis turned the key in the ignition and the radio came on automatically, playing 'Let It Be', sung by Paul McCartney, Nathan's favourite song. Marie went on to tell me that she could feel her son's presence wherever she went. She realised that she would never be afraid of death, because Nathan would be waiting for her.

Marie is not alone in thinking like this. In my experience, the eternal search for answers to why a person took their life leads to an increasing awareness of that person after they have died. Relatives are on alert for songs or symbolic items, such as feathers, butterflies and robins, appearing close by. Whatever a person's beliefs, these signs are a balm to the soul, letting them know that the person is still near them and that one day they will see them again. Sometimes, the human spirit is a remarkable thing.

* * *

The dinner was over, and now we had to find out if the O'Carrolls were interested in helping to run the inaugural

Darkness into Light walk in their home town. It would involve being on the committee and making a commitment – even if it was for one year – to run the event, with all that entailed. In order to differentiate between the various walks around Ireland, the title of each walk would always be 'Darkness into Light' followed by the name of the town or county in which it was being held. It was simpler that way. There was a sense of continuity about it, in particular as the number of locations was growing every year. Here, Marie was to surprise us.

Now, nobody at the table was sure if the walk would work in Killarney, because it had a population of only 13,500 approximately. However, incredible as it may seem, this hard-working town caters for over one million tourists each year. What we did know was that it was a most beautiful setting in which to hold the walk and because everyone knew everyone else, they had a ready-made community that was strong and supportive.

Kieran went on to explain to the group how the walk works, that they would need volunteers on the night so that people could be guided to the start line, they'd need volunteers to distribute t-shirts, to oversee registration, people to choose the route, provide tea and goodies afterwards, and so on. Although Killarney was one of the least populated towns we had dealt with, the workload was exactly the same as with other walks. We had an equal amount of work regardless of the size or numbers. It sounded overwhelming. I remember thinking, how can we expect people to take on this challenge?

I was holding my breath, waiting to hear a no from Marie or Denis, when all of a sudden, in a clear, strong voice, Marie said, 'We will do it on one condition: the walk must be called after Nathan. I want it to be called "Nathan's Walk".'

There was silence. Awkwardness had descended on the group. People were shaking their heads, 'I'm afraid we can't do that, Marie. We cannot allow the walk to be called after Nathan because if that was the case, the whole country would want to call their walk after their loved one who was lost to suicide,' Kieran said gently.

Marie shrugged her shoulders as if this was Kieran's problem. Denis stayed silent. Here was the glimmer of strength and inner determination I'd seen. She looked around the group, her shrug saying it all. 'If it's not called after Nathan, we won't be involved.'

Silence again. 'Well, if that's the case, Marie and Denis,' I said, with equal determination in my voice, 'so be it – it will be known as "Nathan's Walk".'

On the way home from the meeting, Kieran spoke with exasperation. 'We'd break every rule by allowing the Killarney walk to be named after Nathan.'

I knew he was frustrated and I also knew that, unfortunately, it would be he who had to answer to other committees around the country. 'I know, Kieran,' I said soothingly, 'but as we said, we have no idea how long Killarney will run with the Darkness into Light walk. It could be just for one year. And if we can soothe the brokenness of the O'Carrolls by allowing the walk to be in their child's name, then we have done a good job, we have helped a couple and their family divert their grief into the walk. Somehow we will get around the change of name with other committees. You can blame me if there is trouble over it.'

Kieran looked at me and laughed. 'Yeah, right!'

* * *

The special title of the Killarney walk, Nathan's Walk, was accepted by the local community as the right thing to do. The O'Carrolls were well known and liked in Killarney. Marie had that wonderful knack of asking for something and rarely being refused. They organised the first walk to start off in the car park of the Gleneagle Hotel. Their journey would take them down Ross Road, past the historical Muckross Abbey and they would complete the 5-kilometre circuit by returning to the hotel. Tea and coffee, scones and hot dogs would be waiting for everyone, and, for some, a little drop of Jim Beam would be spilled into the hot tea.

For Marie and Denis, the event became a pivotal moment in their lives. In rural Ireland it was still difficult to accept and talk openly about suicide. Yet, the event in 2011 opened a floodgate of acceptance for people who were lost and understanding for those who were in a dark place. Marie and Denis had expected sixty or seventy people to arrive for Nathan's Walk, but that morning every time they thought everyone had arrived, they saw more people coming from all over the town and its outskirts. This was Killarney showing solidarity, openly remembering a little boy and supporting his parents in their attempt to help others. Marie and Denis clutched each other, overwhelmed with gratitude for this huge wave of attendance. Mothers pushing babies in prams, older farmers walking with their dogs on a lead, couples holding hands and middle-aged mums and dads all walked along, murmuring, talking about loved ones who were gone, some crying openly and being comforted by complete strangers.

That dry, cold morning in May 1,500 people turned up. The event was talked about for months afterwards. Marie and Denis became the centre point for the walk, all the time including Nathan's name in their narrative. By the time the walk came around the next year, there was no question that they were going to carry on for as long as they could. The numbers became so big that they could not continue down the Ross Road anymore, because the sheer amount of people was holding up traffic, there was no parking and it was getting a little dangerous. Eventually, Nathan's Walk had to move to the local racecourse.

Immediately after the walk, Denis and Marie would go directly to visit Nathan's grave, telling him that this was all for him. On their way, they would pass Muckross Abbey, whose turbulent history was long forgotten by many. But Denis and Marie knew all about the lone grave at the abbey gate, of the anonymous person who'd died by suicide many years before and was not allowed to be buried on hallowed ground. The O'Carrolls would stop and pray for that soul, too, conscious that no one would be leaving flowers at this grave. As they rose to go and see their son, they were comforted by the thought that from now on, anyone who died by suicide in the county would always be remembered at Nathan's Walk.

CHAPTER SEVEN

The Message Spreads Around the Country

Nathan's Walk had brought the Darkness into Light movement into the south-western corner of the country, mobilising an entire community in support of a grieving family. This story was replicated all over the country during the first ten years of Pieta House. Eventually, there would be over 200 venues, each with its own rationale for doing the walk, each with its own story to tell.

It's often said that if you are going to pay tribute to people, include everyone or no one, because the chances are that somebody will be, or feel, excluded. I would love to mention by name all the men and women around the country and, indeed, in other countries who had the courage and compassion to bring the Darkness into Light movement to their area. Unfortunately, if I did that, this book would be never-ending.

I felt that any tribute needed to capture the early years of the movement, the people who loved what was achieved in the Phoenix Park and whose own personal stories drove them to bring the movement to their own areas. In those early years, the walk was still in its pioneering phase. The original Dublin committee were still learning, but each lesson would be passed on to the newly formed committees dotted around the country. I would like to thank each of these committees for their hard work and dedication. Thank you to those quoted here (some of whom have asked to remain anonymous) for letting me tell their stories and for sharing their own perspectives.

* * *

We first heard from Niamh Connolly in Dungarvan Youthreach in 2012. She was aware of the problems presented by teenage suicide in communities like hers and asked if I might be free to come and talk at a mental health event she was organising. Sadly, I wasn't able to attend, but if Niamh thought that was the last she'd hear from Pieta House, she was wrong. We knew just how important it was to get the message of suicide awareness out there and over the following weeks, I thought about Niamh a lot. I knew from Nathan's story that young people in rural areas often found it difficult to access mental health services. Also, we needed to spread the word about Pieta House.

In 2012 Pieta House was not the phenomenon it is today, and most people in Niamh's area had never heard of it. But the devastation of suicide was, sadly, familiar to too many people. As one committee member says, 'I remember the night I saw Joan Freeman on RTÉ introducing the opening of the first Pieta House centre. The feeling I had watching it was one of relief. I had lost a good friend to suicide and felt at last someone was coming up with a solution to prevent other people from going down this road. I thought to myself, this is one organisation I would be happy to support in some way. Not long after, my childhood, lifelong friend mentioned doing the Darkness into Light walk. I was all on for it and delighted to support it, though I thought we'd be going to Dublin to do the walk, not realising we would go ahead and start one in Dungarvan.'

And start one they did. A few weeks after Niamh's phone call, Dublin committee member Cathy Kelly rang her with a request. 'We don't have a presence in Waterford yet. Would you help us set up a Darkness into Light walk there?'

'But I live in Dungarvan!' Niamh explained, whereupon Cathy cheerily answered, 'Well, sure that's great too.'

Before Niamh knew it, she'd agreed. She'd also agreed to be chairperson of the organising committee, and, as she says, 'One of the most important events in the Déise [Waterford] calendar was born. Over the next ten years, Darkness into Light Dungarvan grew from a humble 300 people on our first walk in 2012 to over 3,000 regular attendees, raising hundreds of thousands of euros, connecting people the length and breadth of the county, and playing a fundamental role in establishing Pieta House in Waterford city in 2016.

'I knew there was a perfect 5-kilometre loop from the Causeway Tennis Club along our beautiful railway track (now the starting point for the Waterford Greenway), which would have wonderful coastal views for the dawn sunrise. I knew I had great friends and contacts to call on to form a powerful committee, and I knew that with the people of Dungarvan, we'd create something special. And we did.'

One of the participants in the first Darkness into Light walk in Dungarvan says, 'It was when numbers were small. It was intimate and it was deeply moving. There was a huge therapy in that walk for me. It was really the beginning of me coming to terms with my brother's suicide, acknowledging what had happened but really for the first time feeling less alone. For the first time, I felt we were not the only ones navigating this traumatic grief.'

Niamh explains, 'The second year of Darkness into Light in Dungarvan was an absolute phenomenon. Word had spread about how wonderful the first walk was, and Pieta's profile had grown nationally. Over 1,200 people took part, and our little town punched way above its weight, raising the most in the country, at over € 40,000. But the tragedy of suicide wasn't abating, and the need for more resources that were easily accessible was undeniable, so we kept working on Darkness into Light Dungarvan.

'More and more organisations and clubs came on board as the numbers grew, such as the Red Cross, Scouting Ireland, Men's Sheds, the coastguard, GAA teams, as well as local schools, businesses and families. Darkness into Light gave people who were devastated by suicide a focus, a purpose and, most importantly, a sense of unity. The connection and warmth experienced at the walks became a balm for their pain, a lessening of their isolation. It gave them a space to talk about their previously unspeakable sorrow. It gave respite to any sense of shame. It gave a light in their previous sense of darkness.'

And it didn't just help the walkers. Committee members were profoundly changed and enriched by their experience, as one committee member explains, 'Then by joining the committee I felt like it was the next step in my therapy. I found huge strength in coming together and working with others, navigating their grief and learning from each other, while also inspired by the people I met giving up their time.'

It was people power in action, Niamh tells me, 'We were just ordinary people, wanting to help, but without any previous experience in running something like this. We both saw and experienced the commonality of struggle. We both witnessed and had to embody ourselves the incredible resilience and bravery to just keep going when you feel afraid that you can't.'

Other committee members felt the same way, 'On a personal level it was like a "coming out" year for me as I had been at home with two small children and not been involved in much other than that. I had experienced social anxiety for a number of years, so it was a challenge to say the least to become involved in a committee and organise a walk. It was a challenge well worth the making and the camaraderie and sense of unity was great, working towards a common cause, one that was dear to all our hearts. It was so nerve-racking the first year and I remember us worrying that people might not turn up at all, so it was a wonderful feeling to see people arrive at the start point.'

For Niamh Connolly, there was a sense that Darkness into Light 'enriched both our personal and our professional lives. It formed lifetime friendships. It took so much work, and a massive amount of energy, but it always gave far more than it took.'

This was felt also by another woman, who shared her experience of this sense of enrichment and how it spread into other parts of her life, 'It helped me so much, from looking deeper into my work [which sometimes involves] attending certain mental health incidents, to dealing with the breakdown of my marriage while tending to a newborn baby. I was able to hold myself in a place that I didn't realise at that time was actually forming the base of a workable relationship with my daughter's dad, despite how difficult it was. Also, not being able to do this [Darkness into Light] without the support of these friends, I have been gifted much more than friendship.'

A couple of years after that first walk, Darkness into Light Dungarvan had outgrown its birthplace of the Causeway Tennis Club. So, even though the club had given the walk such an incredible start, Niamh says, 'We were beyond thrilled when St Augustine's College [also on the coastal path] agreed to host the walk, as it meant our beautiful and now-familiar coastal 5-kilometre route could stay the same. That year, over 3,000 people turned out, nearly a third of the town's population.'

Over the years Dungarvan had groups joining them from all over the area. 'Buses travelling, especially from Youghal, people driving from Carrick-on-Suir, and all over Waterford – we welcomed everyone. Schools made the walk part of their TY experience, or their SPHE curriculum, and the stigma all too common with the word "suicide" was challenged and weakened. Groups sang, individuals spoke, but the heartache of loss was never ignored. Beautiful cherry blossoms have been planted along the walk route in Abbeyside, generously donated, and those bereaved now have a public place to find recognition and acknowledgement of their grief.'

Like many events that start small then grow very quickly, Darkness into Light Dungarvan was not without its challenges. 'Something that grew from so small to so huge was at times hard to manage. Organising a local event, but [one] that was established and run nationally from Dublin, and then regionally from Cork or Limerick, was both wonderful to have in terms of incredible resources, but at times, also difficult,' Niamh explains candidly. 'People not walking on the night because they had no financial means to support the walk, or not being able to buy the t-shirt, that hurt a lot. [We were] trying to encourage the community to be as one, when often the shame of financial means was driving them to the darkness and I felt we were, in fact, excluding some of the ones who needed us the most. But we managed to work through the obstacles, and every year, the feelings of relief, gratitude and immense satisfaction at what we had all achieved inspired us to go again. After all, the event meant so much to so many.'

One participant describes this satisfaction and inspiration, 'I'll always remember those early years, as the crowds gathered and the sense of community, togetherness, compassion and hope that spread amongst all of us there. A unique event, where we stood in the dark in quietness, remembering those who died and walking together in support and love. I loved the drive home after each successful walk, knowing that it had gone off successfully and knowing my little part made a difference. A good feeling.'

Those good feelings were richly rewarded when, in 2014, a group from the Dungarvan committee hopped into their cars and ambushed me and Cathy Kelly in the newly established Pieta House, Cork. I say 'ambushed', but we were delighted to talk to this enthusiastic group, who'd gone to all the trouble of driving to the city to share their passion and their plans. Thankfully, Niamh found me receptive, 'We spent three hours talking with them about the importance of a house being established in the south-east and, in her inimitable style, Joan said, "Okay so", in the same way I had four years earlier.

'Pieta House opened in Waterford city in 2016, and this remains one of the most important and proudest moments in my life – to think that a phone call had started all this! When I look back now, I wonder if I would have said yes so easily if I had known the massive event it would turn into. The work involved. The stress at times. But I knew then, as I know now, that I live somewhere special.

'I remember going around talking to businesses the very first year, and only one person expressed any doubt that the event would take off. They subsequently became one of its best and vital supporters. This represents to me my wonderful community – either on board straight away, or not far off. I knew my friends would help. I knew strangers would help. I'm an optimist and I believe in the goodness in people, despite the hardship of the world, and Darkness into Light Dungarvan has borne this out for me a thousand times. Nothing worthwhile is easy, but some hard work is more worthwhile than most.'

One person with direct experience of the trauma of suicide explains, 'There are no words to define how Darkness into Light supported my personal journey through living with grief from suicide. And continues to do so. But I am very grateful for those walks and for the people who make it happen.'

According to Niamh, 'Darkness into Light is a phenomenon. It brings communities together, it gives comfort to those who need it, and it prevents others from struggling the same way. Darkness into Light Dungarvan has taught me that ordinary people can do extraordinary things. That if you ask, you will receive. If you look for the good, you'll find it. That if you reach out a hand, there is someone there to hold it.'

* * *

Mayo man Alan Gallagher still finds it difficult to talk about the time his niece died by suicide almost twenty years ago. Sarah Louise was only sixteen when she took her life on a cold day in November 2003. To this day the family find it so difficult to accept Sarah Louise's death. She had been troubled for some time, but, as can happen, her poor mental health was missed by the health system. Young girls who take their lives normally take an overdose of tablets and Sarah Louise had attempted suicide using this method before but survived, which should have acted as a warning. She eventually took her life in a way that was fatal, with an act that left no room to save her.

Alan vividly recalls the day when he received a call telling him of the tragedy. He was on his way home from a training session at his local GAA club in Co. Kildare when he got the news. He jumped into the car and went straight to her home on the other side of the country. Her family was utterly broken by her death.

For many years after Sarah Louise died, Alan wanted to find a way to remember his niece and to process the fact of her death, but there seemed to be nothing in terms of an event or ceremony that would really help – until he saw a piece in the paper about Darkness into Light. He immediately rang Pieta House and said he would like to hold the event in Mayo – in six weeks' time!

I had forgotten the remarkable details of this first walk in Mayo, but the memories came flooding back as soon as Alan and I started talking. Alan put together a Darkness into Light walk in six weeks, with a committee that consisted of two people, himself and his wife, Maeve. They lived in Kildare but they were going to hold the Darkness into Light walk in Westport, Co.

Mayo, close to Sarah Louise's home, with volunteers drawn from family and friends. The logistics of this were a nightmare, as he explained to the *Mayo News* in 2017: 'I'm from Achill originally and I lost my niece in 2003 to suicide. It took me a while to get my head around it but I always wanted to help and it took me until 2012 until I could do anything.'

'When we started out, I said if I only helped one person then it's enough for me and obviously we have helped a lot more people judging by the funds and the amount of people taking part. The first year that we set up this walk we had 250 people, which we thought was a lot and last year [2016] we had 1,700 people come to Westport and walk,' Alan said. 'The first year we raised €10,000 and last year we raised over €34,000. It's growing legs each year.'

When Alan called me that first time, he told me he knew of the most amazing place to hold the walk and he had already received permission from the owners. Westport House, then owned by Lord and Lady Altamont, was one of those places that has a combination of grandeur and simplicity. Alan recalls that when he went to the owners, the Brownes, they were immensely helpful. They decided that they could try to track a 5-kilometre walk around the estate, so off they went, walking through fields where cows were munching on spring grass. He was reassured that the cows would not be present on the day of the walk. Lady Altamont even promised that tea and scones would be available for all the participants after the walk was over.

Regretfully, we had to tell Alan that there was no possibility that he could hold the event in such a short time frame. We knew exactly how long the event would take to set up, and it was a lot longer than six weeks.

But Alan was not to be dissuaded. On that first Darkness into Light Westport walk, 250 people turned up in the lashing rain to a windswept Westport House. Before the walk started,

Alan had distributed hundreds of solar tea lights along the path because it was so incredibly dark. They pointed and lit the way towards a little footbridge over a stream, across which people would walk. When the walk was over, Alan and Maeve, armed with large black plastic bags, went out to pick up any rubbish and to collect all the little tea lights. There were none to be found, because people had picked them up on their walk and dropped them into the little stream under the footbridge. This moving sight – hundreds of tea lights bobbing on the water – became a signature piece in the years to come.

Within two years, almost 2,000 people would walk in the grounds of Westport House. As you can imagine, Lady Altamont could not keep up with the number of scones required! And Alan and Maeve? They are still involved in Darkness into Light but, sensibly, have passed responsibility for the organising of Darkness into Light Westport on to someone who actually lives there, instead opting to organise a walk *even further* from their home in Kildare – on Achill Island, where Alan is from and which makes for a spectacular backdrop.

* * *

Eugene and Una Smyth are from Navan. They would be regarded as the 'salt of the earth'. They are humble and unassuming, a couple who thinks and moves as one. They had four children and were united in the way they loved and reared them. Eugene and Una were always encouraging the children to be open about any problems they might have. They had many conversations around the kitchen table, covering topics like religion, social issues such as abortion, sexuality and, of course, they would talk about mental health.

It was because of this openness that one of their children, fifteen-year-old Patrick, disclosed to his parents that he 'didn't feel great'. It was around this time that he stopped going to school; he wanted to stay in his room so that he wouldn't have to engage with anyone. Although Patrick was at a 'rebellious' age, he agreed to allow his parents to seek help for him. As his father later recalled in the *Meath Chronicle*: 'Patrick seemed out of sorts for about a year before he died. He always had loads of friends, was into his practical jokes and excelled at all sports, especially Gaelic and hurling for the local club Clan na nGael.

'It's very hard to explain but we noticed something just wasn't right. He was a bit irrational and often seemed like a different person and he started looking for excuses to miss his much-loved sports. He had also missed a long period at school.

'When he mentioned a few times when he was down that he wanted to "get out of this place", we wondered if he was talking about the house or the town but in hindsight maybe it was something deeper.

'We were afraid to ask the questions in case we pushed him too far or away but once he confided to his sister Stacey (then nineteen) that he had contemplated taking his own life, we knew we had to get him some help.'

Eugene had heard of Pieta House over the years, especially around the time of the Darkness into Light walk every May. He didn't really know what sort of service they provided and when he made his enquiries, he was delighted to know that the charity helped all ages – including teenagers. Diligently, Eugene or Una would bring Patrick from Navan to Pieta House – at first almost every day, then eventually, as Patrick was showing improvement, his sessions became weekly. His parents could see a great change in Patrick: his mood had lifted, he began to go back to school, he started socialising and his bedroom became a place to sleep, rather than a hiding place. Eugene and Una were relieved and as time went by, Patrick had to attend Pieta House less and less. Eventually it wasn't necessary for him to attend at all.

But then, according to Eugene, Patrick seemed to slip and become low again. Within two weeks of his final visit to Pieta House, Patrick took his life. He was a month away from his sixteenth birthday. His death came as a huge blow to everyone at Pieta House. He was so young and had been making such good progress, but suicide is immensely complex and there is no one reason why a person would take his or her life. In our experience, because their brains are still developing, younger people do not realise that the act of suicide is final and fatal, which makes it all the more painful for those who love them.

Over the difficult months and years after Patrick died, Eugene could feel his family floundering at times. He or Una would bring their children, one by one, for support to Pieta House. Like many before him, Eugene knew that his and their grief needed to be channelled into something positive. He felt that they were stuck in a whirl of sadness and, although they were receiving counselling, it was obvious that family members crumbled at different times, usually when there was no therapist around. He knew that this was their journey and that while counselling provided a balm to their raging pain, something all-encompassing for the whole family was necessary. He realised that running the Darkness into Light event in his home town of Navan could be the answer. He was right.

The Smyth family, like so many families who had members attending Pieta House, were always amazed by the fact that this professional, easily accessible, compassionate service was free of charge. During the time Patrick was attending the service, the Smyth family had taken part in different fundraising events for the organisation. Eugene, in particular, did so much. He got involved in gruelling cycles. He climbed Croagh Patrick twice. He felt it was his way, the family's way, of paying back.

When somebody close to them dies by suicide, many families want to hit back, to blame someone, anyone. If anything, the

Smyth family became even more vigorous in their fundraising efforts. They attended every public event that was organised by Pieta House, whether it was a cake sale or the early Darkness into Light walks in the Phoenix Park. They would be the first to turn up every year to the ecumenical memorial Mass that would acknowledge all the relatives of people who died by suicide, as well as remembering the souls who had died in the previous year. Now they were going to undertake their biggest challenge yet, organising their own Darkness into Light walk in their community.

At five minutes past midnight on 4 May 2013, the Smyth family walked calmly out of their house and made their way to Navan Rugby Club for the walk. They had found the perfect venue, a loop that was exactly 5 kilometres around the grounds. Everything was going to plan: they had organised the volunteers, some of whom would man the route, some of whom would register the participants and, of course, the volunteers who, at the end of the walk, would provide sustenance to the walkers. The only nerves that the Smyth family felt were to do with one minor issue – would anyone turn up? They were not disappointed. Navan woke from its slumber and traipsed down to the rugby club. Two thousand men, women and children arrived on that chilly May morning. As Eugene and the family saw the people coming in their droves, he swore softly under his breath, in awe and in fear. Now the nerves were to do with whether they could cope with the numbers!

The event was made all the more poignant because the committee was made up of members of Eugene's family. As well as his wife and children, it also included his own siblings and parents. For many committees like Eugene's, when the walk is over, the committee members meet over breakfast and debrief. This is not an opportunity to say what can be improved, but simply to tell stories about special moments and images of the walk. Everyone has a story to share. In Eugene's case, the sea of yellow t-shirts reminded him so much of Patrick as he watched his friends and neighbours walk with dignity, joyfully talking, sharing, bonding. Una spoke about the Banner of Hope, how she saw people weep as they left loving words of comfort to the person they'd lost. And the children felt that the distribution of the t-shirts on the day and the previous week, when people shared their stories with them, was healing for them all.

The next day, a woman approached Eugene on the street and told him that before the walk she'd wondered how she could bring up the issue of suicide with her children, but that they had the best, most natural conversation on the subject on their way home in the car after the walk. Eugene realised that organising the walk had helped everyone in the family, but also the wider community. Sharing their feelings openly and without shame was so important, as was talking about what had happened to Patrick. Now it was clear that he'd done more than just remember his own pain – he'd helped other people to express theirs and to begin the conversation.

* * *

These people are only a few among many who made a difference to Darkness into Light, bringing it into new locations, giving their all to make their event a success. They would channel their own grief and pain into soothing the grief and pain of others, leading by example, shining a light of hope on so many. These people are extraordinary and, although I am able to pay tribute to only a few, the efforts, dedication and energy of countless others will never be forgotten. Every day, I think of that sea of yellow, marching into the sunlight of a new morning, and I say a thank you to each and every one of them.

Original committee members (from left) Dolores Ronan, Sinéad Ronan-Wells and Avril Copeland with Leo Varadkar

Joan and Pat Freeman

Dolores Ronan,
chairperson of original committee

Photo: Niamh Connolly

The opening of Pieta House in Waterford.
Photo includes suicide prevention advocates Liam
Brazil and Mags Durand O'Connor; Cathy Kelly
(third from left), development director, Pieta House,
and original Darkness into Light committee member;
Lucia Quealy and John McGrath of Terra Nua
construction company; Niamh Connolly (second
from left), Jacinta Mulcahy and Orla Casey of the
Darkness into Light Dungarvan committee; Edel
Spillane and Damien Geoghegan

Photo: Niamh Connolly

Photo: Joey Dunne Photography

Walking for Billy

John Concannon

Tom and Frances Mulligan

Pieta House, Lucan, Co. Dublin

Joan Freeman and John Quinn
following the walk

CHAPTER EIGHT

The Two Johns and the Two Toms

The Darkness into Light walk has always served two purposes: to allow people to come together to remember loved ones in a positive way; and to raise funds. Our service in Pieta House was entirely free to people who sought our help, but in order to provide this free, professional service, we needed the funding to cover our costs. In the early years, the organisation did not receive any state funding and when it did, state funding covered around 10–15 per cent of our costs (in later years, it increased substantially). The golden rule was that we would not allow ourselves to be dependent on this unreliable source, as funding could be pulled at any time. So, our annual fundraiser was not only vital for our survival, it was also the fastest way of promoting the service and for that one day, it would create a blanket of publicity that would cover Ireland.

It was always heartening to see that the message was getting out there. Immediately after the event, people would contact us, asking if they could be involved in the annual walk next year, or to tell us that they were going to do a home-grown event that would help raise funds for us. Without their generosity, we would not have been able to provide a service that is vital for those at risk of suicide. In this chapter I pay tribute to just a few of those who went above and beyond to raise funds for Pieta House, and who swept us all up in their enthusiasm and dedication.

* * *

One person who contacted us in the early years was a taxi driver, John Quinn. I had actually met him not long before Pieta House opened, at a three-monologue play by the Smashing Times Theatre Company in 2005. These monologues were dramatic interpretations, based on the experiences of those who had lost a loved one to suicide. One in particular was that of a young man who described how he spent the last day with a friend who later took his life. I would learn that this was the monologue that had the most profound effect on John.

I had been asked to sit on a panel for a question-and-answer session after the monologues with two other panellists. Even though I was there in my capacity as a therapist, I found it challenging that the questions were mainly from people who had lost someone to suicide. At that point, even though my family had lost someone to suicide, with all of the pain and grief that comes with it, I hadn't gained a huge amount of professional experience in this area and I was nervous of saying the wrong thing. John was one of the first to put up his hand. Without being accusatory, he spoke about the lack of services and asked what, in my opinion, could be done about it. He then went on to reveal that his son had taken his life three months previously, in November 2005. The panel became silent. John continued, saying that if there had been appropriate services available to his son, he believed that Sean would still be alive.

At this point, my plans to open Pieta House had almost become a reality. I had raised the funds to buy a house in Lucan, thanks to a second mortgage on our family home, for our first centre and had employed therapists and counsellors to work there. I told John that Pieta House would be opening in January 2006. This was good news, even though John said aloud what we'd all been thinking: it was too late for Sean.

John and I became firm friends after that night, and over the years, he did everything he could for Pieta House, from bringing catering tins of coffee and teabags, to money that he'd collected in a spontaneous whip-round. His community would organise sulky runs, where young men would race each other while sitting on a shaky horse-drawn sulky (also known as cart or trap). Of course, as they were illegal events, he would only tell me about these fundraising races afterwards! He was loved by all the staff, who would welcome him into the centre, laden down with goodies, swearing like a trooper and yet never offending any of us.

John lived in a socially challenged but close community in west Dublin, an area that would have had more than its share of suicides, especially among young people. John still talks about the night he found his son hanging in their home. He and his wife had been at a fundraising function but had left early because he was worried about his youngest boy. Sean had been a little depressed in recent weeks, having panic attacks and feelings of anxiety. Though he'd been concerned, it had never dawned on John that his son was in danger.

When he pushed open the hall door that night, he knew immediately that there was something wrong. He looked up and saw Sean hanging from the rafters on the landing. John shouted to his wife to call an ambulance and to get a knife. In the meantime, he ran upstairs and pulled Sean's lifeless body towards him. He tried lifting him to take the strain off the rope. It was too late. When the ambulance arrived and the paramedics took Sean away, John screamed until he could scream no more.

After the death of his son, John became the go-to person in his community for people concerned about their children. After Sean's death, even though he had to cope with his own grief and to support his wife and other sons, it was as if he was on a mission, talking openly about the lack of mental health services and helping others. He would receive up to a dozen calls a week and would spend hours at a time talking to the person in crisis.

As Pieta House became more established, he would bring the person down to the centre and wait until a therapist saw them. One day, John was driving his taxi through the estate when a woman ran out of her house, screaming, right in front of his car. He had to swerve to avoid her. She screamed at him for help because her son had hanged himself. John ran into the house and up the stairs to the boy's bedroom. John cut the cord from his neck and began CPR, his mouth covering the boy's lips, blowing as hard as he could while he pushed hard on his chest. He felt the bile spill from the boy's mouth into his own. He thought he had saved him. It wasn't until the paramedic arrived and gently pulled John to his feet that he realised it was too late.

It was a tragedy, and one all too common in this area of the city, where unemployment was high and some young men did not see that they had a future and a place in society. In a short space of time, John Quinn had lost his son and now, this young boy. Both had so much potential and yet they just hadn't been able to see it. John Quinn considered it his personal mission to stop it happening again.

This is how businessman John Concannon came into the life of Pieta House. A Galway man, he'd left school at thirteen to work on the family farm in Tuam. He'd come to fame on the *Late Late Show* in 1987, when he'd demonstrated for Gay Byrne his invention, the Triple Bucket, a simple but clever device that allowed a number of lambs or calves to be fed at one time. People thought that John Concannon was hilarious, but did not take his strange-looking bucket remotely seriously. Little did Gay Byrne, or anyone else, know that his invention would make him a multimillionaire in the years to come.

Unbeknownst to me, John Concannon was filming the programme *The Secret Millionaire*. In the programme, a wealthy person who wanted to help communities and charities would go to live in a deprived area, masquerading as a local person for a week. At the end of the programme this person would reveal his or her identity and would select certain charities or people in the community to help. I was told by the production company that a west-Dublin man would be turning up at Pieta House to offer his services as a volunteer. I've always felt that volunteering is the backbone of any charity organisation, so I was happy to help, not having any idea of John's true mission.

For some reason, John Quinn had been asked to act as a taxi driver and guide to west Dublin for the other John and suggested that he should look at the possibility of volunteering with Pieta House. The programme, which I eventually saw some months later, recorded a very moving scene between the two Johns. They were out for a pint and John Quinn told the Galway man about the loss of his son. He went on to say that he truly believed that if Pieta House had been open at the time of his son's distress, he would still be alive. It was enough for John Concannon to name Pieta House as the charity he wanted to volunteer for.

One morning a film crew arrived to film the 'volunteer' and I was directed to answer the door when this man knocked and I was to bring him into the boardroom and talk to him about volunteering. According to the producer, John Concannon was unemployed and was an ideal candidate for the programme as he was free to volunteer at any time during the day.

When I opened the door to John, I saw a stocky man with a mop of flaming red hair standing on the doorstep. He was wearing tracksuit bottoms and a purple t-shirt that had a dirty big stain on it. I remember thinking that surely the producers could have pointed it out to him or even given him a new one. Although I knew we were to talk about volunteering, for some reason I treated him as if he were a client. I sat close to him on the pouffe while he sat back on the couch. We spoke for two hours, both of us completely oblivious to the cameras. He talked about his best friend who had died by suicide when he was younger, then shared the fact that he hadn't known that the conversation was going to go this way. Then John began to cry. Unsure of whether to continue, I looked at the cameraperson, then back at John. It's always heartbreaking to see people cry about their loss, or their wish to die, but for some reason, I found it more challenging to see this big man crying in front of me, possibly because as a society, we feel that it's not expected of men to express their feelings in this way.

When the filming was over for the day, the producers asked if they could come in again on the Friday to film a few extra scenes. I remember distinctly telling them that it really didn't suit: I was loath to disrupt the gentle ambience of Pieta House and having cameras could put people off. It was alright as a once-off, but I thought two days in the week was too much. They assured me that it would only take an hour and that they would be as unobtrusive as possible. Reluctantly, I agreed.

That Friday morning the camera crew arrived and I remember feeling a little irritated that John Concannon wasn't with them. I was assured that he would arrive any minute. I was instructed to open the door to him again and when I did, I saw John Concannon dressed in an expensive, navy pin-striped suit – grinning. Next to him was John Quinn, who was also grinning! What the hell was going on? My husband would often say to me that I was so trusting and gullible, not only would I swallow a brick but I would swallow a whole row of houses. I was told that the filming was not about volunteering; in fact, the programme was the very first episode of *The Secret Millionaire*.

So, the man who had arrived with a dirty t-shirt on Monday and who was now standing in front of me beautifully attired was a millionaire who was going to donate to Pieta House. Of course, I wept. I was handed a cheque for €25,000 and John Quinn, still grinning, comforted me as he wrapped his arms around me. The cameras would not have caught this but at the same time as he put his arms around me, John Quinn whispered in my ear, 'This guy is going to bring Pieta House to the West.'

John Concannon stayed true to his promise and Pieta House Tuam opened in 2013. In my opinion, it is one of the most beautiful centres in Ireland. It has a 'chocolate box' exterior and the interior is dressed in soothing tones. It was opened there because John Concannon wanted to bring the service to his community. He worked day and night to raise the money for the centre, talking at events and instigating Darkness into Light in his home town. Like John Quinn, this man became the go-to person in the area, whether people were looking for help or wanted to donate. One man left a cheque for €20,000 with John and wept as he spoke about the loss of his daughter. Another older lady donated her week's pension and spoke about her brother who had died by suicide over fifty years before. These were the stories that John listened to almost on a daily basis.

The two Johns kept in touch with each other and with me over the years, attending each other's significant birthdays, welcoming new grandchildren and both celebrating the day I became a senator in 2016.

Looking back, John Concannon and John Quinn were very different people. John Quinn was a Dub through and through, with an accent to match: tough, outspoken, fearless and at times almost blasphemous, yet the most loving, loveable man, or rogue for that matter. John Concannon was a gentle man, with a warm, lilting accent, who had a soft, sensitive soul. On many occasions he would cry at the kindness and generosity of people, and certainly he cried over the tragic tale of the loss of John Quinn's son. Although these two men came from very different backgrounds and had very different personalities, and very different outlooks on life, they had one thing in common: they wanted to save lives.

* * *

Tom Moran and Tom Mulligan also could not be more different. Although both were born around the same time, just like the two Johns, one was brought up in the heart of Dublin and the other was reared in the country, on the border of Limerick and Kerry. Tom Mulligan was a staunch Catholic, who devoted all his life to volunteering. As a young man he had taken a year out of his life to go oversees to help people in the developing world. He had to fund this trip himself and the living conditions were pretty basic. Volunteering was at the core of his life. To this day he volunteers at the Morning Star hostel, who feed poor and homeless men in Dublin's north inner city. Every Thursday you will find Tom in the middle of the soup kitchen, helping the chef and then doling out the food to the men he has come to know by name.

But Tom's volunteering also comes from a different place, one of immense pain and suffering.

Tom is of that generation who went to dances on a weekend night. The TV Club was the place for him and there he met a lovely young woman called Frances. They fell in love, married and went on to have four children. Life was busy for the Mulligan family. Frances worked at the local school, looking after children with special needs, while Tom worked as a facilities manager in the Docklands in Dublin. There, he came to know suicide. On some occasions, as he strolled on the boardwalk in the area, he would witness the rescuing of people who had drowned in the River Liffey, usually through the act of suicide. He told me that one day he found a handbag and opened it up to see if he could find the name of the owner. Inside was a suicide note from a woman who said that she could not take any more of life and asked whoever found this bag to bring it to the local garda station. Tom was immensely sad at this act of loneliness and despair.

Meanwhile, the Mulligan household continued to thrive. The children grew up, and Tom looked on with pride as his only son,

Tomás, showed interest in Gaelic football. As an adult, he became a well-known Dublin footballer. Every game would find Tom Senior waiting on the sidelines, cheering on his son. Afterwards, the two would spend hours analysing the game and performance of the players. Of course, Tom was always sure to praise his son's efforts.

Tom recalls vividly one of the matches his son played against the mighty Kerry: this time the team didn't play too well and they lost. Dejected, they trooped back to the dressing room, their heads drooped, their feet dragging. Tom clapped the back of every one of the team in consolation and in solidarity. As Tomás filed past his father, he told Tom not to wait for him as he was supposed to be going off into town with some of the teammates. Tom smiled and told him to go ahead but to drop home later, because there was bacon and cabbage for dinner and he would keep him some. Tomás never came home.

In the old Harcourt Street Children's Hospital, which was closed a long time ago, there was a ward cruelly named the 'divorce ward'. It was called this because it was filled with unfortunate children suffering from terminal illnesses and, sadly, when they died many of the parents would go their separate ways because they could not comfort each other, each immersed in their own grief.

Pieta House would often counsel parents who had lost children to suicide. We would gently advise them to make sure that they supported and made time for their partner, because during the terrible months of the first year after losing their child, it was easy to lose sight of each other. There were some parents whose mutual support came naturally, such as Johnny and Gertie Fox, Marie and Denis O'Carroll and we also witnessed it with Tom and Frances Mulligan. Tom always reminded me of one of those sword-wielding warriors, ever watchful and protective of his family, in particular Frances. It was my experience that men often behaved like this: stoic, strong, not allowing their emotions to rise to the surface, dealing with their loss in other ways. I think that society often expects this of men and that can be very difficult.

Although totally focused on minding his wife, Tom felt that he needed to channel his grief into something that would make a difference to society and hopefully help to prevent other families going through the same incredible pain. He came up with a cycle race that would take place over two days. On the first day, they would cycle towards Belmullet, Co. Mayo, where Tomás's grandparents lived, and the next day they would head back to Dublin but on a different route. The cycle would end in Crumlin, home town of the Mulligans, and there people would feast on sandwiches and beer, having raised much-needed funds for charity.

The second year of the cycle Tom made Pieta House the recipient of the event's fundraising. Inevitably, I was asked to attend and speak at the function that ended the second day's cycling. In spite of the circumstances, there was much banter and laughter over the shenanigans of the day, slagging the cyclist who was the slowest, or the one who wore flip-flops and no cycle gear.

This became an annual event and I would speak at it every year. I looked forward to it, yet every time I spoke, I would be acutely aware of Frances watching me, waiting to hear her son's name and while I spoke to the audience, I would look at Frances and witness her brokenness. Tom knew that this cycle was raising funds for Pieta House and he also knew it was creating incredible awareness; however, for Frances and their three daughters, it was a constant reminder, a reopening of a wound that would never heal. This cycle, while a magnificent memorial to their brother and son, was also an event they dreaded every year.

* * *

Tom Moran came from a very different background to Tom Mulligan, a small village in Co. Limerick. Drive through Athea and blink once, and you'll have missed it. There were the same buildings as in every small village: a church, a pub and a grocery shop and if you were lucky, there might be a post office. In Tom's village, there was a post office, a grocery shop, a garage and a funeral home – all under the one roof. Tom owned that roof. His children think back fondly to the wreaths that were displayed in the grocery shop windows, the coffins that were stored in the shed at the end of the garden and how petrol and groceries were bought at the same time. Tom was the owner but also the funeral director, dealing with all aspects of the funeral, including embalming the deceased and supporting the family during their loss. Although he had never experienced suicide on a personal level, he was present at all the terrible tragedies of his village and county. It was he who attempted to make the person who had died by suicide presentable, recognisable, and even beautiful. It was Tom who felt the grief while carrying the family through those early days. To this day, the people who died by suicide while he was a funeral director had the most impact on him. He saw the devastation they left behind, the families reeling from the loss, a death that was never accepted, a life that would always be missed.

His memories of the early years of family life and his one-stop shop stayed with him, even when he became an extraordinarily successful businessman, who owned many hotels at home and abroad. As the years passed, he became well known and respected in the hotel business, and eventually throughout Ireland when he opened the landmark Red Cow Hotel on Dublin's Naas Road. The Red Cow became a comforting marker, advising people from the south-west of the country that they had arrived in Dublin but, at the same time, letting them know there was a Limerick man waiting for them.

The Naas Road became a link to Dublin's commuter belt as well as a vital artery to the south of Ireland. Cars, vans and trucks would trundle their way down the busy motorway and when another motorway linked in with the Naas Road, the local authority decided that a roundabout needed to be built to cope with the new junction and the growing traffic. They built this roundabout right outside Tom's hotel. It has, in recent years, become a spaghetti junction because of the volume of traffic. The Red Cow Hotel has become a landmark, and the roundabout is proudly known as the Red Cow Roundabout – but to us Dubs, it is known as the Mad Cow Roundabout!

Tom, who is a gentle, gracious man, married to the lovely Sheila, was honoured by the people of his home county and won the Limerick Person of the Year Award in 2012. But, ever selfless, he decided to put his award to good use by doing something that would link Dublin, where he made an incredibly successful life with his wife and children, and his county of origin, his beloved Limerick, where his life and success had started. He wondered what would be the best way to acknowledge these two counties and the life they had given him but also to do something in aid of a charity. He thought of the people devastated by suicide in the early years and wanted to create an event that would be a memorial to them, while raising much-needed funds for the charity of his choice.

He decided the best thing to do was to walk. He would start in his home village of Athea, Co. Limerick and, for safety reasons, the route would snake its way through the counties of Limerick, Longford, Meath and Dublin. The event was known as the Tomathon. Tom chose Pieta House as his charity because it had a centre in Limerick and, of course, a centre in Dublin. Here again was the link. The plan was that the walk would end on the anniversary of the opening of the Red Cow Hotel. Each day, Tom would walk an average of 20 kilometres and, as the walk progressed, he drew people to him. They followed him, walked with him and gave him money and food. Many were complete strangers and yet they would walk beside him, telling him their stories. Tom would gently nod and listen to another heartbreaking tale.

Tom arrived home to the Red Cow on 16 September 2012, amid the cheers and claps of hundreds of people. The walk was an incredible success, not only because it raised almost € 200,000, or because of the awareness it raised en route, but because it gave people the opportunity to get involved. People from all over the country joined Tom's effort: some would organise walking groups to accompany Tom for short distances, others organised impromptu feeding stations, schools invited Tom to have a photo shoot with them and some people even made their own home-made signposts along the route, showing the way, in a very symbolic manner, for Tom. Additionally, the staff from all of Tom's hotels around the country walked with their boss. In the hotels that were too far away, they set up a Tomathon Walking Machine (a treadmill) and they would spend their free time putting in the steps, so that they, too, were part of the whole adventure.

* * *

Tom Mulligan and Tom Moran came from opposite sides of the social and financial spectrum. While they were very different in many ways, including their personalities, their ambitions, even their builds, they also shared many similarities. They each had a very successful marriage, they were both passionate about their children and they were both hugely involved in their children's lives. I am sure that this can be said about most people, that they share the same core values. However, there was one thing that these two men shared for sure: compassion for humanity.

Although both men had experienced suicide in very different circumstances, they both responded with the same intention, to prevent this traumatic experience happening in other people's lives.

During my time with Pieta House, for reasons of accountability, we needed to break down the cost of providing the service to each individual (remember it was free of charge to the public). We discovered that the cost of treatment for each client, from start to finish, was approximately €1,000. Tom Mulligan and Tom Moran shared a further similarity: they each raised almost €200,000, a total of €400,000. In other words, they saved 400 lives.

CHAPTER NINE

Darkness into Light Grows Legs

The themes that run through this book are hope, strength, resilience and courage. As I have learned from the thousands of volunteers and the energetic committees that steer the annual walks, it is also about bringing the message to as wide an audience as possible. If the Darkness into Light movement spread countrywide, well, why couldn't it spread even further? And with it a message of hope and support for those who needed it most.

Rebecca Skedd embodies all the values that we have come to expect from those who organise the annual walk. When I met her first, in 2013, she was in her early twenties, a young woman from Waterford who came to New York completely on her own. She knew nobody, but that didn't daunt her: she found a job at the New York Irish Center, she found accommodation and she found her sea legs helping the emigrant Irish community in that vast city.

She quickly found that the community needed help in the mental health area, as she told me, 'I first heard about Pieta House, Darkness into Light and, of course, Joan Freeman, through social media during my first year living in New York. Being from Ireland and living 3,000 miles away, meant, of course, that my social media and my interests were always very attuned to what was happening in Ireland. Working in the Irish Community Center here in New York, my role was focused primarily on what the Irish diaspora needed, as well as identifying what support services were lacking. If you were suicidal, if you had no health insurance, if you had no family, it was simple: you had nowhere to go. It was difficult to comprehend, but there was a massive void in mental health services in this city, and yet Pieta House [could be] available at no cost, to not only the Irish community, but anyone who didn't have health insurance or a salary that would allow you the luxury of paying for private services.'

Like Dublin and some other cities, New York's mental health provision was the Cinderella of the health service. The approach to both suicide and self-harm was primarily a medical one. Following a suicide attempt, or if a person was in mental distress, they would be admitted to a psychiatric hospital for a mandatory amount of time (usually seventy-two hours). It was even more difficult if you were undocumented. Without health insurance, without family and with the fear of being caught out all the time, New York can be a very lonely place for immigrants.

Rebecca has a warm, friendly and bubbly personality and it helped in her bonding with Irish emigrants that she had an Irish accent. New York really does live up to the clichés: it's the city that never sleeps, a place in which you can either make it big or become lost and alone. When you arrive in New York, it can be a very lonely time, especially in the beginning. You have no idea the relief people feel when they ring the centre and are greeted by an Irish accent. You suddenly believe that you are with one of your own.

Rebecca quickly learned that many members of the Irish community in New York were struggling. 'During my first year working in the Irish Center, and before Pieta House came to New York, we would have a lot of enquiries from people desperate for help. There seemed to be a wide range of presenting concerns, from loneliness to suicidal ideation.

Whether it was the person themselves calling, or a loved one on their behalf, desperate for answers, help, or guidance, we couldn't do anything for them. Those phone calls were the most difficult to listen to: it was such a challenge and so incredibly disheartening not having anywhere to send them. What do you do? There wasn't really anything, at that time, that we could do. The situation was fairly dire; something had to change. Any life lost as a result of the inaccessibility of services was a life too many. We needed to be proactive and we needed to do everything we could to bring about change.'

Homesickness was a constant theme among the emigrant Irish. The Irish Center would hold a lunch every week for the older Irish members, of which Rebecca was the star. They adored her. She was a link to home, especially because many of them hadn't been back to Ireland in decades. When I attended ones of these lunches at Rebecca's invitation, it reminded me of the times that my parents would cry when we were living in England as they sang hymns and folk songs, because when Rebecca spoke to these people in the Irish Center you could see a wistfulness and a longing for Ireland in their eyes. As the child of emigrants myself, I understood that longing.

Rebecca knew that action needed to be taken and quickly. 'It was 2014, and I thought to myself, what if I just reached out to Pieta House and see if we could even do a Darkness into Light walk here, surely that would help highlight the need for such services in the Irish community. It would bring awareness, it would bring us together, but most importantly, even if it just helped one single person, it would mean the world.

'I sent off an email to the generic email address I found on their website. I can wholeheartedly say I did not expect a response. However, within twenty-four hours, I had an email from Joan Freeman. "When can I come over and meet you?" it said.

'I actually couldn't believe it, I was hoping to do a walk here but from Joan's email, it immediately sounded like so much more was about to happen. I reckon we spent weeks cleaning the centre up in anticipation of her arrival. We genuinely just couldn't believe that the founder of the organisation was coming over to meet us. That is one of many testaments to who Joan Freeman is.

'It couldn't have been more than a month before Joan came over. I remember the day so vividly. She swanned into the centre with such vibrancy, but from the minute I started a conversation with her, it was her compassion and sheer passion that struck me the most. That, and her bravery. "If there's a need, why don't we just open a centre?" she said. "We absolutely must do what we can to help the Irish community living here." And that we did. Joan was, and still is to this day, the most warm person I have met. There's something about being in her company that just feels like home.'

I am flattered by Rebecca's description of me, but really, it was her can-do attitude that brought me over to New York in 2014. Here was a young woman who wanted to start a Darkness into Light walk in this huge city. The problem with New York is not only the vastness of the city but also the spread of it. Unlike Boston, where much of the Irish community is located in one area of the city, in New York, the Irish population is spread right across the city, so it was difficult for Rebecca to try to pinpoint the best place for the walk. You might think that Central Park would be the perfect place, but for people to go there at 4 a.m., and by subway because there was no parking, would just be too dangerous. So, the most likely place to hold the walk was in an Irish setting and where better than Gaelic Park, which is located in an Irish area in the Bronx.

Even at the beginning, the thinking was that this venture would eventually grow legs; that, as in Ireland, the Darkness into

Light walk would take place at different venues in the years to come. New York was too broad and too big to have just one venue. However, none of it would have happened without two crucial things. The first was Rebecca: her energy, enthusiasm and her ability to connect were crucial elements in the mix. The second was that we were dealing with an Irish community that, although spread out, is incredibly tight knit. The moment you arrive in New York and meet up with an Irish person, you really are at home. The Irish are renowned for their generosity, but that generosity knows no bounds when the Irish help the Irish in New York. And, just like Ireland, everyone knows everyone else.

The idea of Darkness into Light in New York was so exciting, not only for the staff and the board in Pieta House Ireland, but also for the Irish in New York.

Rebecca selected her own committee members, who were as dedicated and committed as she was. This might surprise you, but I have never liked going on committees because they tend to fall into the same potholes: you have the Talker, the Know All, the Doer, the Non-Doer, the Absent One and then you have the poor unfortunate chairperson who is trying to hold it all together. I'm aware that this sounds so ungracious, because I know there are thousands of committees who do the most marvellous work, but that's been my experience of the dynamics. In stark contrast, all the Darkness into Light committees were extraordinary. There were no slackers, everyone was passionate about what they were doing and everyone had a job they were responsible for. There was a sense of solidarity, a oneness, a sense of belonging. People felt that they were almost family. Like every family, I am sure they wanted to kill each other at times!

As in all the other Darkness into Light walks, consistency was the order of the day. Rebecca made sure that the template of the walk was replicated in every way, not only in the t-shirts, but also the tea lights, the Banner of Hope and, of course, the cup of tea after the event. Naturally, the committee were afraid that people might not turn up on the morning. I think Fear (with a capital F) is probably the most shared emotion in the days and hours before a walk. All committees are terrified that no one will show up, or that someone will get hurt, or that the t-shirts won't arrive on time. The moment the last person crosses the finish line there is an enormous sense of relief. Many committee members feel a huge sense of anticlimax when the walk is over too, probably because they have been living on adrenaline for weeks and they have to wait until next year for that same buzz. As Rebecca explains, 'Hurdles, barriers, complications – there wasn't any difficulty we weren't faced with. And to this day, I know that that first year is a testament to the strength and resilience our organisation so proudly wears today.'

According to Rebecca, the walk is important because, 'I think suicide is something that strongly impacts everyone, entire communities even. I know that every suicide that has happened here, among the Irish, sends shudders right throughout the community, whether you knew the person or not. Although dispersed across a massive city, the community here is tight knit and because most people do not have family here, your community, your circle, immediately becomes your family; your home away from home. And every suicide feels personal, it feels preventable. You wonder, what could I have done to help that person? What if there were services available to help them?

'Of course, stigma was another hurdle we had to overcome, or so we thought. In 2015, when we decided to proceed with a Darkness into Light walk, our committee wondered if people would even show up. It was such a genuine fear. Even though we had been working so hard, and reaching out to vast amounts of individuals, clubs, associations, you name it, we were fearful. And wow, I will never, ever, forget the morning of the walk. There was, of course, hype in the days leading up to the walk, but absolutely nothing could have prepared us for what was to come.

'We showed up bright and early, had our checklists, our volunteers, our t-shirts laid out and ready to go. Within minutes of arriving, the floodgates opened and a sea of people started to pour into Gaelic Park. We were inundated with registrations, but the buzz was just phenomenal. As we prepared to blow the starting whistle, a few members of the committee and myself took a second together and we started to cry. It was dark, but all you could see was literally a thousand yellow bodies in front of you, ready to walk in solidarity. It was so incredibly overwhelming.'

But as Rebecca candidly acknowledges, 'It hurt a little bit too; it brought the raw reality to the surface. You knew that every single person gathered there, in the middle of the night, in the rain, was there for a reason. And while many were walking to offer hope and to support loved ones and friends, the majority were walking in memory of someone they had lost, or were in despair for someone they knew they were losing. And it made me realise that as a community here in New York, we needed more. We needed somewhere for people to turn when they had nowhere else to go, we needed a service that was confidential, non-judgemental and oozed compassion, care and understanding. And the very people who were going to support this centre and make it happen were the very people who were walking at 4 a.m.

'This walk meant the world to me. It was the starting point for something truly incredible. Emotions ran high, but there was a sense of energy that soared through participants that was so comforting, creating such a strong sense of togetherness, even if you walked alone. I am so grateful for what this experience provided; it allowed people to openly grieve and honour a loved one, it offered so much hope, it was a testimony to the strength and resilience of the Irish community, and it brought so many people together in solidarity to diminish the stigma that surrounds suicide and mental health. The messaging couldn't have been more clear: it's okay not to be okay, and it is absolutely okay to reach out for support when you need it.'

Rebecca is completely right, and her thoughts on the walk echo those of so many who have lost loved ones to suicide. The symbolism of the tea lights, the brightness of the t-shirts and their message of hope was so clear, but most of all, the heartfelt messages left from walkers on the Banner of Hope. 'There were messages of pain and despair, mixed with hope, optimism and the emphasis that you are not alone. Even the messages of hurt offered companionship. Grief is the most lonely feeling in the world but knowing someone else is also grieving and feeling your pain provides a sense of togetherness. For some people, it was perhaps the first time they have felt such inclusivity. And that alone made the walk the most powerful gesture imaginable.

'Another moving moment, or several, was the conversations that followed the walk, not only directly with me, but by witnessing groups of people talking, reflecting, sharing and offering compassion and empathy towards each other. It was so uplifting and empowering. They say a problem shared is a problem halved, yet so many of us tend to suffer in silence, and similarly, can grieve in silence too. When attempting to explain grief, or express your feelings, it's easy to assume that no one will understand. This walk gave people an opportunity to share. It prompted people to open up, and in doing so, they found quite the opposite; people do understand, people feel what you feel, they, too, are consumed by grief. And the consolation of knowing that you are not alone in your feelings offers even the smallest amount of comfort.'

* * *

Of course, Darkness into Light in New York was a huge success, but the extra success was that it brought the Pieta service to the city. The board of the Irish Center were more than accommodating in allowing Pieta House to set up in their premises, the New York Irish Center Building in Long Island City, Queens. Following in-depth discussions, it was decided to set up a pilot programme introducing the service to the city for a year. This was a success and demand grew, so the service was made permanent. Thus, Solace House was born in this magnificent building that the members of the board bought through a mortgage and were religiously paying back each month. This first centre opened in Long Island City in 2015, followed by another in 2017 in Yonkers, an area with high levels of drug abuse and deprivation.

Even though the names of the centres in Ireland and America were different, the same therapeutic model was used, the same Mrs Doyle 'go on, go on, go on' approach to providing a warm welcome and, of course, the same compassion. Rebecca puts it better, 'One thing Joan emphasised to me, over and over again, was the utmost importance of making someone who is in need or struggling feel at home. Whether you achieved that by offering them a cup of tea (crucial in Joan's eyes) or how you approached and spoke to them, it was more critical than anything else. And in New York, more so than anywhere else, that meant more than anything. Feeling homesick can be so overwhelmingly consuming. And, of course, being so far from home and from family, a very common and totally normal emotion to feel. It is almost an instant relief when someone shows compassion and understanding. This was one of the things we embedded into the structure of our services, a simple gesture at the core of our beliefs, and it had such an impact on everyone who walked through our doors.'

Again, when people began to ring the new centre, the Irish accent was the most comforting and soothing thing they could have heard. Without knowing, we created a slogan totally by accident. Whenever Rebecca or I gave talks to different Irish groups, we would always say, 'We are here to look after the Irish wherever they are.'

What was most interesting was that almost 60 per cent of people who attended the service were of other nationalities, highlighting the gaps in mental health services in the city. Once again, it was down to the generosity of the Irish that everyone was welcome, because the chairperson of the board, Pat McGowan, insisted that this service be open to everyone. His attitude was that this city, this country had provided work and a future for thousands of Irish, it was now our turn to give back.

In time we were approached by the New York Department of Education, who expressed an interest in our approach. In New York at the time, if a school discovered that one of their pupils was self-harming, their parents would be notified immediately and they would have to bring their child to a psychiatric unit, where they would be assessed and more than likely detained. The child could not go back to school unless they were given permission by the unit and their stay would remain on record for their whole life, which prevented them from working for the government, in the fire service or police, for example.

In Pieta House we understood that a child who self-harms is not attempting suicide; they are communicating their distress through their body, usually because they don't have the vocabulary or ability to put that distress into words. We learned that this was something new and radical for the New York Department of Education at that time, but we were delighted to share our philosophy of hope and faith in young people and in their ability to overcome challenges.

Everything in New York costs a fortune, so you can imagine that running a free service was extremely expensive and yet it was down to the generosity of the diaspora that every penny needed to run the centres was found. Thanks to Rebecca, the board and, of course, all the people who volunteered, whether it was on reception, the cup of tea or fundraising, the service in New York not only survived but thrived where so many exported businesses and services fail.

Although it was physically and emotionally challenging for me during those three years of going back and forth to New York, I am also grateful for it, not just because of the people I met but because I witnessed first-hand what it is to be an Irish person abroad. We are loved. No wonder 34.5 million Americans claim they are Irish. Sometimes, this could be quite entertaining, as when I interviewed a man who was applying for a job as a therapist in the New York centre. When I asked him (his name was Sean) if he was from an Irish background, he immediately nodded his head and said he was living with this girl whose great-great-great-grandmother was Irish.

Very soon Irish communities in other parts of the United States wanted their own Darkness into Light walk, so the walk began to spread across America, with venues in Boston, Chicago, Philadelphia, San Francisco, Texas, and more venues in New York. The same enthusiasm and energy seen in Ireland and in New York was being repeated again and again. It was contagious. All down to the heroic work of Rebecca Skedd, a young woman from Waterford, who not only had a great love for humanity but also a great love for the Irish – wherever they are.

CHAPTER TEN

Standing on the Shoulders of Giants

It is still hard to believe that Darkness into Light has been such a success and while so much of it is down to the passion and enthusiasm of the ordinary people of Ireland who drove the spread of the movement, credit also has to be directed to certain professionals and organisations who brought Pieta House and the walk to the next level.

I met Cilian Fennell at a workshop that he was giving on storytelling and communication. He was mesmerising; he had such a command of the language and words would pour out from him in his soft, lilting Galway accent. With a background in television, producing the *Late Late Show* with Gay Byrne, he knew how to use stories to help people connect and inspire them to action. I knew we needed someone who could put a different slant on the messaging around suicide and Cilian, with his expertise and enthusiasm, seemed just the person.

When I originally opened Pieta House in 2006, it was the first service to provide clinical intervention to those who were in suicidal distress. Three years later, in 2009, we held a Darkness into Light walk, also a first. However, by 2011, suicide and mental health was spoken about more, especially by celebrities, and by 2013 there were 300 other charities in this area at some level. Most of them had started because of someone's own personal experience of losing a loved one to suicide. The challenge was to differentiate Pieta House from all the other charities and to shift the dialogue around suicide to one of hope. So, we engaged Stillwater, a communications company owned and run by Cilian and his sister, Natasha, to help us to rise to this challenge.

Stillwater had watched the Darkness into Light initiative grow; they saw the potential to establish this as Pieta's flagship event, by creating a campaign that would reach into every county in Ireland, a campaign that was based around hope and connection. Although each year the walk was gaining momentum, Stillwater saw a clear opportunity to grow the event further. They also recognised that Pieta House and the Darkness into Light walk needed a different level of scale, energy and funding. We needed a sponsor. This sponsor would not only provide funding but would deliver increased engagement and even more exposure.

Securing a sponsor was essential to achieving the reach and objectives of this ambitious campaign. In 2012 London hosted the Olympics. As a neighbourly gesture, they had invited people in Dublin to run with the Olympic torch, as an extension of the relay through Northern Ireland. Each runner was to carry the torch for 300 metres and among many guests, both sporting legends and local heroes, Electric Ireland gave me the honour of running through some of the city's streets with the torch. It was such a momentous and exciting time. Everybody I met wanted to hold the torch and to be part of the occasion. Afterwards I was invited to lunch by two of the directors of Electric Ireland, Bríd Horan and Pat O'Doherty. Both reflected the ethos of their organisation, which had deep roots in the community. The company was committed to playing a role in addressing some of the key social issues that faced Ireland. Suicide was one such issue. During that lunch the seeds of Electric Ireland's sponsorship of Darkness into Light were sown. By 2013 the organisation was fully behind the Darkness into Light campaign, not only providing financial support that allowed us to promote and expand the walk, but also involving their own staff, many of whom volunteered on the morning and many more promoted the event in different towns across the country.

One of Stillwater's cleverest ideas was to have launch events in every county in Ireland, which they called the 'Whistle-stop Tour'. Approximately three weeks before the walk, I would travel around the country to prearranged venues, launching the event in that area, meeting the committees and then I would be interviewed on local radio. The watershed year for the event was 2013: there were twenty venues around the country and the Phoenix Park witnessed 7,000 men, women and children take part. A video was made with Kathryn Thomas providing the voiceover. I will never forget her opening words: 'At 4 a.m. on a chilly May morning, the darkness was interrupted by an incredible sound and a spectacular sight.'

It was around this time that social media took off, and it was wonderful to be able to harness its power to promote Darkness into Light. However, with new venues and many new requests to host a Darkness into Light event, we realised that we needed staff to coordinate what was fast becoming a year-round task. Two people became heads of this staff and developed Darkness into Light into the incredible movement it is today, Kieran Brady and Marie Peelo.

Kieran Brady, the local auctioneer who had advised me to start a charity, agreed to join the board of Pieta House in 2006. Within a couple of years, he became a staff member, overseeing the accounts and funding for the organisation. Around the same time, a new volunteer named Marie Peelo joined, originally helping Pieta House at reception, handling the phones and putting new clients at ease. For her own personal reasons, Marie wanted to work for Pieta House. She was one of those people who could put her hand to anything and also had an incredible way of dealing with people. Everyone she met felt her warmth and compassion. Marie eventually became a member of staff and was a natural candidate firstly to deal with all the volunteers and then to join Kieran in heading the Darkness into Light initiative.

They made for a dynamic duo. Before Kieran took over, we had six venues around the country. His fearless goal was to double it. Both he and Marie would visit the new applicants for the walk and help them select a suitable 5-kilometre route. They empowered every committee they dealt with. As the years passed, they realised that they could not keep up with the expansion by themselves; so, their team grew. Staff were allocated to the four provinces and became responsible for the walk's growth in their areas. The expansion was not just limited to Ireland. Soon it became an international event with venues all over the world, from Taiwan to Dubai, each event coordinated by Irish people living in the area. There was a Rebecca Skedd behind all the international walks, Irish people who, like Rebecca, kept one eye on their country, who still wanted the connection with home.

It was wonderful to see the images of Darkness into Light walks around the world on social media, the first walk taking place almost a day before ours, in Australia. For most of the hours before and during the walk, Pieta House would be trending on Twitter. People across the globe were linking in with each other, sharing their grief, and yet providing hope. Each year would see not only new venues appearing across the world but the numbers in the Phoenix Park expanding, until the crowds became too big to handle. O'Connell Street and the Quays became a glorified car park in the early hours of the morning. People would have to walk nearly 5 kilometres before they even got to the start line. So, the Phoenix Park as Dublin's solo venue had to change. Soon, places such as Skerries, Bray, Maynooth and other towns and villages around the city were hosting the walk. Darkness into Light had grown and expanded beyond anyone's wildest dreams.

Social media was unheard of when Pieta House opened its doors in 2006. Not alone was there no such thing as Twitter, most people did not have a mobile phone; in fact, hard though it may be to believe now, the iPhone only came on the market in Ireland in June 2008. Most people also did not have computers or the internet in their home, so social media and building a website for Pieta House were the last things on my mind. My daughter Marie, however, had other ideas. She was working in Pieta House at the time and she fell in love with and married Ian Cumbers, who was an expert in all things digital. Ian became the digital coordinator of Pieta House at just the moment when social media became popular in Ireland. It was the perfect storm. With the combination of our brand new website, our Facebook page, which attracted 30,000 followers in its first month, as well as the emergence of Twitter, Darkness into Light exploded online. On the morning of the walk, Ian and Marie would head to the Darkness into Light Bray venue, but they couldn't take part in the walk because they were on their phones all the time responding to messages on behalf of Pieta. In later years, they had to sit in front of their laptops for the whole night, trying to manage the social media presence of Darkness into Light.

In 2015 there was a crowd of 12,000 people in the Phoenix Park, waiting patiently for the signal to begin walking. The crowds behind the start line were backed up almost the whole length of Chesterfield Avenue. It took some walkers at the end of the crowd twenty minutes just to get to the start line. There are usually runners who want to take part and are the first to go off – and they had completed their run by the time the last of the walkers stepped over the start line! The finish line was no better: a backlog of people formed as they tried to walk across the line while taking selfies to show everyone their achievement. Social media had not only helped us to spread the word about Darkness into Light events, it was also helping people to connect and to spread Darkness into Light's message of hope.

* * *

In January 2015 I stood down as CEO of Pieta House. This would be the last year in which I was involved in Darkness into Light and it was the last time I would address the crowd. It was hard to believe that this had all happened because of a chance meeting with a young woman on a plane. I still keep in touch with Maria. She still completes marathons every year and, of course, runs them in aid of different charities. Companies sponsor her because of her passion for humanity.

The original organising committee of Darkness into Light has changed slightly over the years. Dolores Ronan is still chairperson, she volunteers with Pieta House and plays an integral role in the Darkness into Light team. Her daughter Sinéad works for Pieta House. Johnny and Gertie Fox still fulfil their roles and look forward to the event for months. Johnny has starred in lots of advertisements for the walk. He has also been on the *Late Late Show* talking about his son, which is incredibly powerful viewing. Although Avril Copeland and Suzanne Graham have retired from the committee, they still carry out their duties each year. Marie Peelo and Kieran Brady have retired from Pieta House. Thanks to their work, there are now 200 venues across the world participating in Darkness into Light every year.

Marie and Denis O'Carroll, Eugene and Una Smyth, Niamh Connolly, and Alan and Maeve Gallagher are all still involved in the walk, still giving their time and energy and love for the cause. I want to thank all the people in my life who said yes, starting with Dolores Ronan and the rest of the committee, and eventually the thousands of volunteers and walkers across the world, each one saying yes to the phenomenon that Darkness into Light has become.

* * *

It was difficult for me to walk away from Pieta House and Darkness into Light. I often thought that running Pieta House was like a relationship between a parent and a truculent teenager: watching with joy and fear as this child grows up, wanting them to be independent, but at the same time not wanting to let go.

I stood down for a few reasons. Firstly, after nine years, with ten centres established and the Darkness into Light movement in full swing, I felt I had brought the organisation as far as I could. It was time to pass it on to someone else with new energy and the skills to run what had become a nationwide organisation. Secondly, I was given the opportunity by the board of Pieta House to look across the pond to America and start an organisation there. I would not have been able to run Pieta in Ireland and start fresh in New York at the same time.

The third reason I decided to step down was because I was afraid of catching 'founderitis'. When founder's disease, founder's syndrome, or whatever you might call it, strikes, the drive, vision and characteristics that are crucial to a company's initial success as a start-up can become a hindrance to its maturation and development. It is a common problem when an organisation grows bigger, and one I was eager to avoid. It was imperative also that when I stepped down I did not go on the board of Pieta House, because I could be still directing from the sidelines.

The first couple of years after I stepped away were quite difficult. Although I was still pursuing the possibility of opening in New York, unfortunately, for legal reasons, I could not bring the name 'Pieta House' to America. That was when I felt most alone. I was used to having the support of the executive team and the board of Pieta; now I had no one. Although I was still employed by Pieta House, my role was difficult to define. Eventually, I saw myself as an ambassador, a person who would try to promote the service at home and abroad. As time went on, however, it was obvious that the role of promoting the service lay with the new CEO and my engagements became fewer and fewer. When I was chosen to be a senator, originally I saw it as a wonderful opportunity to promote Pieta House and issues around mental health inside government walls, though it quickly became apparent that I needed to break away completely from Pieta House because it was causing confusion, to the staff and to other organisations. Despite remaining as a senator for four years, I grieved over the loss of my beloved Pieta House.

Writing this book has brought up all the sorrows and joys of my work with the organisation and with Darkness into Light. I interviewed many people asking for their recollections and their reasons for joining this ever-expanding movement. One person I really wanted to ask to contribute was my husband, Pat. I asked if he would like to write about his experiences over the years, not just because he was involved in the early days of Darkness into Light but also because he had witnessed the creation of Pieta House and saw all the challenges and stresses I went through while running a charity, as well as celebrating its successes with me. The piece he wrote was all about me. It was loving and moving and he spoke about me with great pride. There was no way I could include it, of course, but reading it made me realise that Pat is the real hero of the story. Right from the beginning, Pat stood by me: when I came up with the plan to open a service for people who were suicidal; when we remortgaged our house; when I was absent from him and the family, both physically and emotionally. He went to all the events that I had to go to, even though I knew, deep down, that there were many he did not want to attend.

I often used Pat in a light-hearted way as part of the speech that I would inevitably have to deliver at functions. I would tell the audience how most people, when they enquire about Pat, put the word 'poor' in front of his name, and how we are married forty years and I always tell him that they have been the happiest forty years of his life. People would laugh at this, but I can imagine that there were many lonely times for him. We never had a holiday in the early years of Pieta House, and when we eventually did, although I was physically present, my mind was elsewhere, always focused on the organisation. I never realised at the time, but this must have been difficult for him. This chapter is called 'Standing on the Shoulders of Giants'. I'm referring to our sponsors and supporters, Electric Ireland and Stillwater, and, of course, to the staff, clients and volunteers of Pieta House and Darkness into Light – but, most of all, I'm referring to standing on the shoulders of Pat. Without his support, none of this would have been possible.

Afterword

The morning of the tenth anniversary of Darkness into Light is etched into my memory. I joined an army of thousands as we gathered in the Phoenix Park.

All across the pathways and fields, lines of brightly coloured t-shirts moved like threads of light through the early morning darkness as they made their way to the start line.

It is an extraordinary sight to see so many people gathered in this way, shrouded in the darkness of a May morning and united in a common cause. Similar scenes were being enacted in villages, towns and cities across the country.

Strangely, although the grief of suicide was the common factor, my overriding memory of that morning was the positivity of the participants, all determined to raise awareness and bring hope to those who have been impacted by suicide and self-harm.

As we journeyed through the park, and as the darkness was slowly replaced by the light of a new day, names and pictures started to emerge from the darkness, printed on people's t-shirts – tributes to those who could not be there that day. I remember being particularly stuck by a little child, wearing a t-shirt with the words: 'I'm doing this for my dad.'

We walked for them all that day.

Hundreds of thousands have walked into the sunrise since the initial spark was lit in the Phoenix Park in 2009. Darkness into Light has realised the desire of Irish people to connect with their communities and spread a message of hope. For so many the walk has become an annual event in their calendars.

The success of Darkness into Light is by no means accidental. None of this would be possible without the individuals who put up their hands and committed to organising each event – some with very personal reasons for choosing to do so.

It requires months of preparation and planning by a dedicated team of volunteers, many of whom do so year after year. Each one has contributed to making Darkness into Light a global message of hope.

As the pandemic hit and we advised people to stay apart, this team of volunteers redoubled their efforts. They recognised that for many, the isolation and stress of the pandemic would take a toll, and that the need for critical services would be even greater. Volunteers found new ways to share that sunrise moment and to raise the vital funds which enable Pieta to be there for people in crisis.

Over the years, Darkness into Light has gone from strength to strength. Irish people continue to express their gratitude in their thousands. Personally, I am truly grateful for your extraordinary work and for the privilege to have walked alongside some of you.

Leo Varadkar
Tánaiste

Acknowledgements and Remembrance

'Death is not extinguishing the light.
It is putting out the lamp because the dawn has come.'
Rabindranath Tagore, writer and artist

Grief is as unique as you are, and as individual as a fingerprint. Being bereaved by suicide has been described as 'grief with the volume turned up'. People may make assumptions that only close family grieve; however, many people can be affected. You may be the close friend of the person, a work colleague, or maybe you have been professionally involved in helping before or after the person died. I know we grieve in Pieta House. We form an intimate bond with the person that we are trying to help and support, and if this person goes on to die by suicide, the loss is immediate and extraordinarily painful, not just for the therapist who works with that person, but for all the staff members who provide a welcome, answer a call or give a cup of tea.

For obvious reasons this book cannot include all the names of people who died by suicide over the years, but we want to acknowledge them. Thank you for coming to us in your hour of need. Thank you for allowing and including us in your life. However long or short our relationship was with you, I promise – you will never be forgotten.

To all the people who have participated in the Darkness into Light walk, I know that the majority of you are there because someone close to you has died by suicide. It is so difficult to know how to memorialise someone who has died in this way. The grief is different. But I believe there is only one way to mourn a loss such as this that may ease or sooth the brokenness and that is to grieve together. The time to do it is a bitterly cold morning in May, at 5 a.m., just as the dawn is about to rise and the first rays of light are peeping through. This is the time you should look around at all the people who surround you. They are walking with you and for you. They understand the sorrow that you are going through because they have gone through it too.

Finally, to the people who contributed to this book. My heartfelt love and appreciation to Johnny and Gertie Fox, Marie and Denis O'Carroll, Eugene and Una Smyth, Alan and Maeve Gallagher, Niamh Connolly, Tom Mulligan, Tom Moran, John Quinn and John Concannon. You, and the hundreds of people like you, put your own sorrow to one side in order to reach out to others. The death of your loved one has saved many lives because you became the voice of the families and friends who were bereaved through suicide. Not only was your voice for them, but you forged a path that would provide comfort and solace on their journey while endeavouring to provide protection to all families in the hope that this tragedy would not end up at their door. I want to say thank you not just from myself, but also on behalf of my country.

Robert and Fergal Fox
(sons of Gertie and Johnny Fox)

Nathan O'Carroll
(son of Marie and Denis O'Carroll)

Patrick Smyth
(son of Eugene and Una Smyth)

Sarah Louise Gallagher
(niece of Alan and Maeve Gallagher)

Tomás Mulligan
(son of Tom and Francis Mulligan)

Sean Quinn
(son of John and Renee Quinn)

Beloved Friend
(of John Concannon)

The people of Athea, Limerick and surrounds
(Tom Moran)

Finally, to Rose and Eugene Smyth, who died recently
(parents of Eugene Smyth)

My thanks to those who helped with the publication of this book: Taoiseach Micheál Martin; Tánaiste Leo Varadkar; Dr Harry Barry; Joe Houghton; photographers Joey Dunne and Gary Ashe; Ivana Bacik TD; Aoife Roantree and all the team at Dubray Books; David Carroll; Natasha Fennell and Rebecca Bury from Stillwater; Daragh Reddin; Alison Walsh; Colette Dower, Leeann Gallagher, Pamela McLoughlin, David Macken, Aoibhín Browne, Andrea de Angelis Rego, Sean Stilling, Mark Howard, Tony Moroney, Síne Quinn and all the team at Beehive Books.

Once again thanks to Dolores Ronan, Cathy Kelly, Sinéad Ronan-Wells, Suzanne Graham, Avril Copeland and Johnny and Gertie Fox, heroes of the first Darkness into Light committee. Of course, to all the staff of Pieta House who work so tirelessly every year supporting and caring for the committee members, in particular to Marie Peelo and Kieran Brady. And finally, to Maria, the very first piece of this incredible domino effect.

Support

Feeling alone or afraid? Worried about a friend or a family member? Here are some support services that can help you.

Pieta
Pieta provide free counselling to those with suicidal ideation, those engaging in self-harm, and those bereaved by suicide. Staff are fully qualified and provide a professional one-to-one therapeutic service. A doctor's referral or a psychiatric report is not required.

- 24-hour crisis line. Please call 1800 247 247 or text HELP to 51444
- To make an appointment, please call 0818 111 126

Samaritans
The Samaritans telephone service is available 24 hours a day and provides confidential and non-judgemental support.

- Freephone 116 123
- Email jo@samaritans.ie
- For details of your nearest branch, visit www.samaritans.ie

Childline

A support service dedicated completely to children.

- Freephone 1800 666 666
- Free text the word TALK to 50101

BeLonG To

A support and information service for LGBTI+ young people.

- For details of youth work, education and training, visit www.belongto.org
- To contact a youth worker via text, email and phone, visit www.belongto.org/we-are-here-for-you/
- Crisis counselling service. To book an appointment free of charge, please call 01 462 4792 or email belongto@pieta.ie